Petite Style

Petite Style

The Ultimate Fashion Guide for Women 5'4" and Under

SUSAN LUDWIG

WITH JANICE STEINBERG

ILLUSTRATIONS BY BARBARA RHODES

NAL BOOKS

NEW AMERICAN LIBRARY

NEW YORK AND SCARBOROUGH, ONTARIO

TO DICK
with all my love

Published simultaneously in Canada by The New American Library of
Canada Limited.

 NAL TRADEMARK REG. U.S. PAT. OFF. AND FOREIGN COUNTRIES
REGISTERED TRADEMARK—MARCA REGISTRADA
HECHO EN CHICAGO, U.S.A.

SIGNET, SIGNET CLASSIC, MENTOR, ONYX, PLUME, MERIDIAN and
NAL BOOKS are published *in the United States* by
NAL PENGUIN INC., 1633 Broadway, New York, New York 10019,
and *in Canada* by The New American Library of Canada Limited,
81 Mack Avenue, Scarborough, Ontario M1L 1M8

Library of Congress Cataloging-in-Publication Data

Ludwig, Susan.
  Petite style.

  1. Clothing and dress.   I. Steinberg, Janice.
II. Title.
TT560.L83   1988   646'.34   87-28106
ISBN 0-453-00586-1

Designed by Barbara Huntley

First Printing, April, 1988

1 2 3 4 5 6 7 8 9

PRINTED IN THE UNITED STATES OF AMERICA

CONTENTS

ACKNOWLEDGMENTS

Just as one develops a personal style over time, so too was this book written. I've been guided, encouraged, and assisted by many along the way and I've enjoyed every step. My deepest thanks to each of you:

✳ Judith Adams, for urging me to embark upon this project in the first place.

✳ Milane Christiansen, owner of *The Book Works*, who first heard my concept, believed in it, and introduced me to my agent and friend,

✳ Sandy Dijkstra, to whom I am indebted for her astuteness, enthusiasm, and tenacity in making this book happen.

✳ My editors, Alexia Dorszynski, Carole Hall, and Helen Eisenbach, without whose insight, professionalism, and nurturing this book would not have been realized.

✳ Barbara Rhodes, whose illustrations capture perfectly the beauty of petite women.

✳ Barbara Huntley, for her sensitive and conscientious book design that only serves to enhance my message.

✳ Richard Neil, for his camera work and enthusiastic support.

✳ The late Jeffery Garrett of Personal Appearances and his able, creative staff: Elaine Rosa, Shannon Kitzman, Bill Reyes, Linda Severino, Taula, and Edward.

✳ The four beautiful women who had the courage to undergo a complete makeover: Jaye Blackwood, Claire Pavich, Ruth Vanderford, and Tené Villanueva.

✳ The representatives of manufacturers and stores who assisted me so generously, especially Robbi Kraft of Bullock's, Carole Trilling of Karen Austin, and Vilma Boettcher of Brazilian Flavor.

✳ The members of Petites Unlimited, for their friendship and lovely examples.

✳ The countless petite women who have contributed to my philosophy of Petite Style, each one a woman to look up to in her own way, especially Mary Ellen Drummond, Elaine Ireland, Toni Peetoom, Nancy Soulé, and my models, Lorrie Ball, Suzanna Krebs, Beca Lewis, Karen Rockwell, Adair Sirota, and Connie Turner.

✳ My husband Dick, for his love, support, and absolute patience throughout this entire process.

✳ My parents, Charles and Ethel Bodell, for their love and encouragement, so instrumental in forming my basic belief that small is beautiful.

S.L.

Petite Style

My special thanks go to Jack Cassidy, for his unfailing support, encouragement, and ability to make me laugh; and to two petite women who have inspired me—my grandmother, the late Dora Scribner for her strength; and my mother, Harriet Steinberg, who taught me to love the written word.

J.S.

INTRODUCTION

The Petite Style Promise

"How do you do it?" women ask me. "How do you look so put together?" . . . "You always look so chic!" . . . "Can *I* learn to dress like that?" I am stopped by women asking questions like these at work, in the supermarket, at restaurants. I love to hear them, and to share what I've learned from a lifelong fascination with style—the textures, shapes, and colors of clothes . . . the way couture and what's worn on the street come together as Fashion.

At 4'11", I've enjoyed using my creativity to adapt the latest styles to flatter my petite frame. I've been fascinated by the under-the-skin aspect of style as well—the self-confidence it takes to make a fashion statement *and* the confidence that comes with making heads turn. When a woman offers me the sincere compliment of asking my advice to help her develop her own unique style, I have so much to tell her! I barely begin and two hours have passed. Hence this book . . . so I can tell you everything I've learned.

"Susan, do you remember our Christmas skirts?" my sister Leslie asked me last week.

Thirty years have passed since we proudly wore those red felt skirts, each adorned with a green Christmas tree. But I will never forget them.

One of my fondest childhood memories is of having clothes sewn for me. For very, very special occasions, my mother took Leslie and me to a seamstress we affectionately called Nana. Nana (who was actually named Mrs. Sandburg) inhabited a magic realm of shiny

1

scissors, pins stuck into a plump apple cushion, dozens of spools of colored thread, and soft, wondrous fabrics. My mother would take me there for several fittings. Once, when I had been studying the metric system in school, Nana asked where I wanted her to hem a skirt. "Make it one centimeter longer," I said, provoking gales of laughter from her and Mom. Made with the extra care of custom sewing, Nana's clothes *felt* special. Even at six or seven, I relished the idea that Leslie and I had clothes like no one else's! In addition to the Christmas skirt—the tree was decorated with sequins and beads to look like ornaments—I remember a soft velveteen princess-style jumper in blue that I wore with a pink organdy blouse. I still treasure the buttons from that blouse—pearly white, edged in gold, and each hand-painted with a pink rosebud.

Nana made sewing look like fun. So one day when Janice Pearlman stood up in front of our third grade class and asked if anyone would like to take sewing lessons with her, my hand shot up. But what a difficult beginning I had. I started with doll's clothes, not realizing they are some of the hardest things to sew because they're so small. My father got me a full-size sewing machine, but to operate it, I had to hand-turn a crank at the side! Finally, Dad no longer worried I'd hurt myself, and he attached the pedal so I could operate it electrically. The first garment I made for myself was a red-and-black plaid skirt. I didn't know a novice seamstress should never start with plaid, which is hard to match.

But I persisted. By the time I was in high school, I was making almost all my own clothes. In fact, half of my high school wardrobe came from the remnant table at Marshall Field's. It took forty-five minutes by bus and subway for my mother and me to go from our home in northwest Chicago to Marshall Field's State Street store. What anticipation I felt as we neared downtown! From the Field's remnant table, I fed my craving for unusual fabrics. I couldn't afford to make a whole dress out of an exotic fabric, but it was easy to find enough remnant material for a blouse or a skirt. After I'd absorbed color, mood, and excitement in the fabric department, Mom and I had lunch in Field's Walnut Room. I'd return home exhilarated, carrying my bag filled with silks and printed wools, and dreaming of what to make from them.

By designing clothes, I was developing a sensitivity to fabric, texture, color, and how garments are put together . . . and I was creating one-of-a-kind garments that I still think of with excitement. One Easter I built my outfit around a gift I'd received—vintage gloves made of soft pink leather. I made a gray sheath in one of my favorite fabrics, raw silk. For my Easter bonnet, I bought a hat form at Fishman's in downtown Chicago, covered it in dusty pink fabric, and trimmed it with silk flowers. I completed the outfit with dyed-to-match gray heels. It was a simple, elegant ensemble. I'm convinced that simplicity always stands out. Prom dresses in the 1960s abounded with ruffles and frills. But when I designed my own prom dress, I chose raw silk in a luscious chartreuse. Floor-length, with a scooped neckline in front and back, it was fitted all the way down, with an over-bodice

2

Petite Style

that gave a blouson effect. "Elegant simplicity" became my watchword. It still is.

I continued to sew while I studied for my education degree at the University of Illinois Chicago Circle campus. When I married Dick at the end of my junior year, I designed my wedding dress. Soon I found myself adjusting to marriage, my own home, a new city (the Navy sent us to San Diego), and my first full-time job. I nearly forgot about style. Besides, my job as an elementary school teacher required clothes that could withstand clutching, fingerpaint-smeared fingers, chalk dust, and sitting on the classroom floor.

After Dick left the Navy we returned to Chicago, where I taught school and earned my M.A. in education . . . and where for three years, we dreamed about balmy San Diego. Finally we packed up and headed west. It was the first time we had chosen a place to live that wasn't determined by our families or Uncle Sam. Armed with my M.A., I accepted an exciting high school position, administering new programs and teaching human relations courses. I felt energized and confident . . . and I rekindled my love affair with style. I sewed whenever I found time—elegant, tailored designs—and I applied my sense of fashion to dressing every day. My female colleagues and my students kept asking how I looked so chic . . . and if I could help them look more put-together.

Four years ago I took the plunge and founded a company to help people present themselves with confidence and impact. I wanted a name for my business that was uniquely *me* . . . that reflected my love of fashion *and* my belief that style comes from within, as well as from outward appearance. I chose the name Heightened Image.

It was a lucky choice, because Karen Rockwell saw my flier at a petite fashion sale and invited me to help her start a club for petite women. The concept intrigued me, and soon we attended a planning meeting with two other women. After marveling at the fact that we all stood eye-to-eye (a revelation!), we got down to business. Why would petites want to meet? we asked ourselves. What common interests would bring petite women together? At that high-energy meeting, we listed self-defense, health and fitness, and my special interest, communication. And of course, we came back again and again to *fashion:* Where to find petite-sized clothing, pantyhose, and shoes; the trick to accessorizing; how to enhance a total image via makeup and hair.

I realized that although women of all heights had been asking me to help them look good, I had something special to offer petite women. When I sewed I customized my clothes to my figure, my coloring, my personality, and of course, my 4'11" height. Over many years, from my very first plaid skirt, I had been developing a sense of style that applied particularly to petites. I had learned to adapt the fashion trends I saw in magazines, to alter ready-made clothing, and to work with accessories. Did other petite women—not just the handful at our planning meeting—yearn for that kind of information? I was about to find out that indeed, they did. At our next meeting, each of us brought a few friends; then they brought more petite women. Soon we were taking a room in a restaurant!

3
=========================

The Petite Style Promise

Petites Unlimited, as we call ourselves, now attracts 300 women to standing-room-only fashion shows. They come to see petite-flattering looks . . . on real, live petite models! The idea of using petite models occurred to us when we were planning a fashion show with Robbi Kraft, the 5'3" publicity director of Bullock's. It took us by storm. Petite models? Of course! In fact, how could we show petite fashions on anyone else? No matter how well a garment might suit a petite women, if she saw it on a 5'7" model she would have an underlying doubt about whether it would look good on her. We recruited some of our own members to model. The audience response was fantastic, and several of our members have now signed with modeling agencies!

Yes, style *can* be learned.

I have seen exciting changes in hundreds of women who have cultivated Petite Style. They are dressing with verve—wearing simpler, more elegant clothes, more color, more accessories. They've come into their own. Now they tell me women are asking them the same questions I've always heard: "How do you look so put together?" . . . "How do you look so great?"

WHO IS PETITE?

I sometimes hear the mistaken idea that "petite" refers exclusively to women who wear the smallest sizes, such as size 2 or 4. Short women who are voluptuous may not think of themselves as petite. However, I consider any woman to be petite if she is 5'4" or under. While petites have many individual body types, we all share a very important quality—height. Any women who is 5'4" or under will benefit from applying the same fashion principles, whether she is boyishly slim, seductively curvy, or somewhere in between. As you will see, these principles offer an enormous amount of freedom with which you can express your individual style.

THE PETITE STYLE PROMISE

As I developed my own style and worked with Petites Unlimited, I've given a great deal of thought to what distinguishes the woman with Petite Style.

I've seen that style is unique for every woman—that's one of the things I like best about it. The woman with Petite Style is an individualist. Her style also goes beyond fashion. It's feeling good about herself and projecting a sense of confidence. I think there's a special energy and zest for life that comes with being petite and confident. The woman with Petite Style projects that energy and zest in her attitude toward clothes.

✳ The woman with Petite Style dresses with a unique, individual flair—whether she is attending a business meeting or sipping wine at a romantic summer picnic.

✳ She looks forward to shopping as an opportunity to develop new combinations and learn about the latest fashion trends. She knows where to find petite-proportioned clothes and how to make them fit perfectly.

✳ She presents a polished appearance by making the most of her figure, features, and hair.

✳ She makes an impact on the world. She uses the power of style to project authority, flatter her femininity, express her artistic side.

5
════════════════

The Petite Style Promise

The woman with Petite Style . . . will be you. I assure you, style can be learned. And I will show you how to create *your* Petite Style, step by step.

We'll start by understanding the concept of longitude, the basis for petite-flattering fashions. You will discover how three fashion elements—line, proportion, and balance—affect you as a petite, and how you can make these elements work for you.

You've undoubtedly heard innumerable rules as to how petites should dress. Some are valid; some are not. As we build on your knowledge of longitude, you'll learn how to break the rules and still look great. You'll find many wonderful looks you thought you couldn't wear.

I call accessories the petite's best friend. Accessories add excitement and pizzazz; they're a major contributor to Petite Style. We'll talk about what to look for in each type of accessory, then discuss how and when to accessorize, and what goes into a basic accessory wardrobe.

Once you have learned about the basic fashion elements, rules, and accessories, I'll help you apply that information to your own wardrobe. You will discover many new, exciting looks hanging right in your closet and identify your most important shopping needs.

The next step is mistake-proof shopping. Knowing how, when, and especially where to shop is essential to having Petite Style. I'll tell you what to look for in terms of fit, what to ask yourself before you buy, and where you can find hard-to-locate items like petite coats and shoes.

Once you make a purchase, you want it to look perfect on you. With a little help, even an inexperienced seamstress can perform image-flattering alterations. I'll help you decide whether to do an alteration yourself or take it to a tailor. And I'll show you how to achieve a couture look, whether you choose to alter ready-made clothing or sew your own.

An added benefit of Petite Style is to draw attention to your figure assets and minimize figure problems. I'll give you suggestions tailored to your individual proportions.

To complement your distinctive dress, petite-flattering hair and makeup techniques will lend the finishing touches to your polished look.

You'll look wonderful and feel confident. Intangibles such as voice and body language are also vital to your total image. I'll show you how to make an impact on everyone you meet by cultivating the style and authority that come from within.

As you follow these steps, you'll also meet many stylish petites, including four women who underwent complete makeovers.

I have met and heard from hundreds of petite women, and I've found that virtually all of them agree with me: Being petite is wonderful. "I feel like a diamond—tiny and exquisite!" Rory (5'1") wrote to me. Marianne (5') said, "Being short has required me to develop my personal power—and allows me to express it."

We enjoy being small because we feel feminine . . . because people find us approachable . . . because we like to surprise people with our strength . . . and of course because petite women have a special appeal to men! Being petite makes us feel unique and special. I hope that *you* feel the same way. I promise that you are going to feel and look your best as you discover your one-of-a-kind Petite Style.

Petite Flair

How to Create It

CHAPTER 1

The Beauty of Longitude

For the petite woman, the key to looking great is a single word: *longitude.* When you understand longitude, you will always look your very best. To give yourself a visual image of longitude, imagine holding a wide rubber band, one end in each hand, and moving your hands apart. As you stretch the rubber band, it appears longer and narrower. That elongated look is longitude. You can achieve a similar effect with your clothes. The result is long, luscious . . . and wonderful.

You can create longitude by applying just three basic fashion principles: line, proportion, and balance. These three principles will take the guesswork out of your shopping and dressing each day. Despite the changes in fashion from year to year, you will always know what looks good on you because line, proportion, and balance never change. In this chapter I'll show you how each of these principles affects you as a petite, whether you're wearing a sophisticated evening gown or a funky thrift-store ensemble.

To learn how you can create petite-flattering longitude with line, proportion, and balance, let's consider them one at a time.

LINE

Every outfit comprises several lines, which may be vertical, horizontal, or diagonal. Understanding how line can create longitude is one of the most important principles of Petite Style.

The eye is attracted to line and will follow wherever a line leads it. The eye obeys the *dominant* line—that is, the line that garners attention because it is longer, wider, brighter, or repeated more often than any other. Thus a garment with dominant *vertical* lines will give you longitude, whereas dominant *horizontal* lines will make you look shorter. To gain maximum longitude, you could try to eliminate every horizontal line from an outfit. But there's an easier, more stylish solution.

The savvy petite doesn't avoid horizontals—she judiciously allows verticals to dominate.

As for *diagonal* lines, they are neither purely vertical nor horizontal. Whether they flatter the petite depends on the angle and length of the line. Generally, the longer the diagonal, the more longitude it will give you.

In this section you will learn to recognize several kinds of line and use them to your advantage. Let's look at line created by color, "built-in" features, detailing, and accessories.

Dominant vertical lines add longitude.

Dominant horizontal lines make you look shorter.

Diagonal lines can be flattering.

Color and Line

Color is the first thing people see when they see you. Imagine I am walking toward you, wearing a peach blouse and peach skirt. As I approach you, your eyes glide over my silhouette. Seeing my matching blouse and skirt, you perceive a long vertical line of color: I've created longitude. If, however, I am wearing a white blouse and black skirt, these large blocks of contrasting color divide me, "chopping" me up. The image is not as pleasing to the eye—nor as flattering to me. (See photographs in insert.)

That is why petites are often advised to wear the same color top and bottom. One continuous color from shoulder to hem creates a vertical line. Monochromatic outfits—such as jumpsuits, dresses, and skirts or trousers with matching jackets in a single color—are indeed petite-flattering. They give you a long line of color from shoulder to hem.

However, you don't have to wear the *identical* color throughout the torso. The following tips will give you more color options:

✳ You won't sacrifice longitude when you wear colors from the same family (beige, brown) or colors of similar intensity (pastels *or* brights). Low-contrast colors will produce an elongating effect similar to a monochromatic outfit.

✳ You will also look great in contrasting colors, as long as the dominant line is vertical. I'll wear a navy skirt with a fuschia blouse *under* a navy jacket. The navy on top and bottom creates a long line that is reinforced by the vertical column of fuschia showing from the blouse.

✳ Another tip for wearing contrasting colors: You'll gain longitude when you repeat the accent color throughout your silhouette. For example, with the outfit I've just described—the fuchsia blouse with navy skirt and jacket—you might add fuchsia earrings and shoes. Then don a navy hat with a fuchsia pin for maximum flair.

✳ Avoid wearing strongly contrasting colors, such as a yellow blouse and navy skirt, however. Blocks of high-contrast color cut the torso in half. They are too choppy for a small frame.

Built-In Line

Line is not just created by different colors. Even solid-colored garments have line. Wherever there is a seam or an edge, you have a built-in line. This subtle but very important line can profoundly affect the way a garment looks on you.

✳ A one-piece princess-style dress with long, prominent seams creates an unbroken vertical line—as opposed to a peasant-style dress with horizontal seams at the shoulder yoke and the waist and in tiers on the skirt, which creates a dominant horizontal impression.

✳ The closing edge of a wrap dress creates a long diagonal line from neck to hem that flatters the petite figure.

✳ The front closings of jackets, coats, and cardigan sweaters also provide built-in verticals.

✳ The wise petite will capitalize on fabrics with built-in vertical lines, such as ribbed knits, corduroys, herringbones, and cable knits.

✳ Don't overlook the line of the silhouette: A silk crepe body-skimming dress creates a more pleasing vertical line than a stiff taffeta dress with a full, gathered skirt that stands away from the body.

✳ The vertical of long sleeves looks better on the petite than short, puffy sleeves.

The longer the diagonal the better.

Note the verticals—jacket edge, cable knit.

Petite Flair

ABOVE *Full volume, in skirts and sleeves, and stiff fabric, such as taffeta or corduroy, detract.*

LEFT *Body skimming garments enhance the natural vertical of the silhouette . . .*

Detailing and Line

From my years of sewing, I'm very sensitive to line added by detailing such as buttons, collars, pleats, topstitching, or trim. Each of these sounds minor, but they can make a big difference in longitude. Look for those that emphasize the vertical, such as:

✳ A skirt or dress closing with buttons running from neck or waist down to the hem

✳ A V-neckline complemented by a Chelsea collar

✳ Flanging (vertical tucks) at the shoulder of a jacket or dress

✳ Braid added to the front edge of a Chanel-style jacket

Note the verticals—pleats, button closing . . .

. . . flanging at the shoulder.

A petite can wear a yoke at the shoulder, which creates a horizontal line, when the rest of the garment gives a vertical line. However, be cautious of:

* Yokes at the hip
* Flounces or ruffles
* Borders or bands of color at the hemline
* Bands of contrasting color at mid-torso

Accessories and Line

With any outfit, you can choose from dozens of accessory possibilities—and every accessory affects longitude. Consider the verticals presented by a trailing scarf, a long necklace, or the shoulder strap of a purse . . . versus the horizontal lines created by a belt or a short, chunky necklace. As I mentioned earlier, the trick isn't to shun all horizontals but to *emphasize* the vertical when you accessorize.

For an easy demonstration of how accessories create line, put on a blouse, leaving the top two buttons undone, or wear a top with a V-neckline. Add a long necklace or a long scarf and appreciate the flattery of that vertical line. Now, for contrast, try a choker or a scarf tied in a fifties style. It breaks up the vertical of your V-neckline. Notice the immediate shortening effect on your neck. I don't believe in many rules, but you should *never* interrupt a long, flattering V-neckline.

Beware of dominant horizontal lines—hip yoke, bands of color, hemline flounce.

A long necklace extends the flattering neckline.

Never interrupt a long, flattering neckline with a short, chunky necklace.

Although a belt presents a horizontal line, wearing a belt in a similar color to your dress more than makes up for the subtle horizontal by adding polish to your ensemble. When you wear the belt under a third layer, such as a jacket, you still have a dominant vertical line.

Your legs will look longer and slimmer when you key your hose to your hemline—dark hose with a dark skirt, light hose with light—so your legs and torso present a continuous vertical color line.

BRING THE EYE UP!

Want a sure-fire way to create longitude? Make the most interesting part of your outfit the part around your face. Enjoy dangling earrings and colorful scarves. Look for dresses with detailing at the shoulders. You will gain longitude, attention . . . and Petite Style.

PROPORTION

Petites who want longitude must pay attention to proportion—the art of scaling clothes to the figure. Proportion is related to line, in that your body presents a natural vertical line. By keeping clothes in proportion, you're taking advantage of that natural vertical. There are three elements to proportion: fit, prints and plaids, and fabric.

Remember our rubber band at the beginning of this chapter? Proportion helps create the effect of the rubber band at its longest and most stretched, as you'll see when we discuss how to make each element of proportion work for you.

Pattern at the shoulder brings the eye up.

WOMEN TO LOOK UP TO

Natasha Josefowitz is proudly entering her sixties as a business professor, management consultant, and published poet. She writes a syndicated column published weekly in over one hundred newspapers. The 5'2" Ph.D. is a nationally recognized expert on women in business and the author of *Paths to Power: A Woman's Guide from First Job to Top Executive*.

Frequently in the public eye as a lecturer, Dr. Josefowitz prefers simple styles and vibrant colors: "If I wear a neutral suit, it will have something special about it, a bright blouse or a pin. I want to walk into the room and not fade into the woodwork."

Fit and Proportion

Clothes that fit proportionally follow the natural vertical of the body. That's why proportional fit is so critical to longitude . . . and why you need to know what constitutes good fit for petites, and to insist that you get it in your clothes. Petites tend to have narrower shoulders, shorter arms, shorter legs, and shorter measurements neck-to-waist than taller women. In terms of fit, we need:

✳ Jackets with shorter sleeves

✳ Pants with a rise (crotch seam) that doesn't go to our knees

✳ Smaller buttons and pockets

✳ Narrower collars and lapels

✳ Higher armholes

✳ Pockets intended to appear at breast or hip that do just that

Our garments should hang smoothly with sufficient ease of movement and style. In the immortal words of one of my favorite petites, Mae West (5′), "I like my clothes to be tight enough to show I'm a woman, but loose enough to show I'm a lady."

When fashions feature drop shoulders, batwing or dolman sleeves, low waists, flared pants, or anything oversized, fit can be tough. But don't despair. *As a petite, you can wear any of the style trends, as long as the fit is proportional to your figure.* Often you can make a trend petite-proportioned by doing a simple alteration, such as tapering a seam in flared pants or batwing sleeves. If a jacket comes with shoulder pads fit for a linebacker, you can easily substitute smaller pads. (You'll find out how to do many simple alterations in Chapter 6.)

17

Petite Flair

Petite Style demands petite proportion.

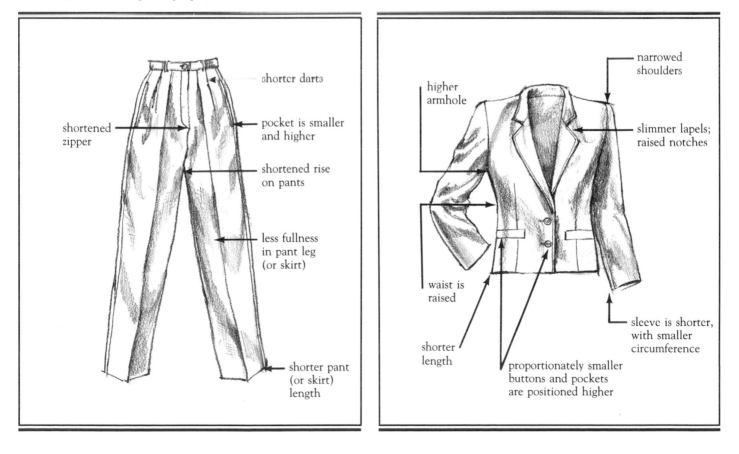

shorter darts

pocket is smaller and higher

shortened rise on pants

shortened zipper

less fullness in pant leg (or skirt)

shorter pant (or skirt) length

narrowed shoulders

higher armhole

slimmer lapels; raised notches

waist is raised

shorter length

sleeve is shorter, with smaller circumference

proportionately smaller buttons and pockets are positioned higher

Prints, Plaids, and Proportion

How boring fashion would be if we had only solid-colored clothes to choose from! I find great fun, excitement, and mood-enhancement in paisleys, florals, geometrics, and dots. Prints and plaids, proportioned to our petite frames, infuse an outfit with flair. Avoid too-large prints that can be overwhelming—you want to wear your clothes, not let them wear you! To maintain longitude:

✳ Keep prints in proportion to your petite figure. In general, the print should be no larger than your hand.

✳ Consider the size of a print in relation to the size of the garment. A widely spaced floral print may look attractive on a mid-calf-length skirt. Shorten the skirt and the print may look overwhelming—out of proportion to the amount of skirt. Try to visualize the end results

*Keep prints
in proportion . . .*

*. . . a small print
flatters the
petite figure.*

before investing time and money in alterations. (In the next chapter you'll find some guidelines on skirt length.)

✳ As you pull one of the colors from a print to repeat in a solid, be sure the solid color balances the print. A boldly printed blouse in emerald, magenta, and gold needs similarly bold pants—say in the emerald—rather than in a soft green.

✳ Since plaids contain horizontal as well as vertical lines, they are best worn by a slender petite—often to her advantage, as the plaid lends substance, counteracting the impression that she may blow away. For more longitude, select plaids with dominant vertical lines.

✳ Since plaids attract the eye, I prefer to wear them on the upper torso—in a jacket, cape, or scarf. By wearing a plaid on your lower body, you run the risk of broadening your hips—never *my* first choice—and bringing the eye downward.

WOMEN TO LOOK UP TO

When *Harper's Bazaar* selected "America's 10 Most Beautiful Women" in 1986, *three* of them were petite: First Lady Nancy Reagan and actresses Lisa Bonet and **Priscilla Presley.** Priscilla, who plays Jenna Wade on TV's *Dallas,* is 5′4″. She maintains her weight at a svelte 110 pounds through a combination of careful eating, weight training, and her favorite exercise, karate! She proudly holds a brown belt (just one below the highest, black belt). When it comes to fashion, she says, "I hate styles that are restrictive or uncomfortable, but I have to watch proportions carefully."

Fabric and Proportion

My personal heaven has got to resemble a giant fabric store. I could get lost among silks, wools, and linens for eternity. Fabrics come in such a wonderful variety that every petite can find fabrics that please her eye and flatter her proportions. However, not all fabrics meet the test. Some present too much stiffness or too much bulk for petites to carry well. Like too-large prints, they can drown you. Choose fabrics that will flatter, such as:

✳ Fabrics that drape, flow, and hang softly on the body, such as knits and crepes

✳ Smooth, lightweight fabrics, such as gabardine, cotton, and silk

✳ Natural fabrics, such as cotton, silk, wool, linen

To avoid being overwhelmed, steer clear of:

✳ Stiff fabrics, like taffeta and brocade

✳ Bulky fabrics like mohair or terry cloth, or any heavily textured fabric or knit

✳ Fabrics that reflect light, like satin and velour, as they tend to make you look heavier

Choose soft, draping fabrics.   *Avoid those that are stiff or bulky.*

I've developed a list of fabrics with notes about how flattering each is for petites. When you shop for clothing or fabric, keep in mind that no list is definitive, because so much depends on the actual garment, the style, and the figure of the wearer. (See pages 22 and 23)

BALANCE

Balance is an important concept for the petite woman who wants longitude and a polished, attractive appearance. Balance means that each element of your outfit complements the others, creating harmony and interest. Think of balancing opposites: rough texture with smooth; fullness with slimness. With a little time—and some experimentation in front of the mirror—you can train your eye to recognize balance in the shapes, colors, patterns, textures, and finishes of your clothing and accessories.

You have probably sensed the need for balance at some time. When was the last time you dressed, looked in the mirror, and felt something wasn't right? Did your outfit need something *more,* for emphasis? Did it need something *less* (understatement is often the key to elegance)? Did it need something *different*—a heavier shoe or boot, more color around the face, a more attention-getting pair of earrings?

You'll achieve a polished look when you focus on two things: balancing your upper and lower torso, and balancing the components of your outfits.

Balance Upper and Lower Torso

You gain longitude when you balance fullness on the upper *or* lower torso by wearing more form-fitting clothes elsewhere. Consider your silhouette, from top to toe, when you look in the mirror . . . and remember that, in general, you want to "bring the eye up" for more longitude.

✳ Balance a black, white, and yellow floral skirt with a black intarsia sweater that has a yellow and white floral motif repeated at the shoulder.

✳ A long jacket with a long skirt may cut your height. Create balance with a shorter jacket.

✳ Do you have a favorite big, blousy top? Balance the fullness of the top with fitted pants for maximum longitude.

✳ Exercise moderation. A glittery metallic gold knit evening top with a matching skirt is *too* much for the petite. For balance, pair the top with a black gored skirt in crepe de chine.

Balance Components of an Outfit

Opposites attract. And by deftly weaving opposites into your ensembles, *you* will attract attention with a polished, harmonious appearance. Think of this principle as push/pull.

✳ Subdued/bright: Balance a somber navy suit with shiny bright gold jewelry. The jewelry will give life to the outfit.

✳ Print/solid: Pair an intricately patterned top with a plain skirt. You want the top to get all the attention it deserves.

Fabric	Good for Petites	Wear with Caution	Stiff	Bulky	Reflects light	Feminine	Tailored	Casual	Comments
PROBLEMS FOR PETITES						**OVERALL LOOK**			
Angora		X		X		X			Fluffiness makes it soft to touch, but gives illusion of bulk; sheds silky hairs on dark colors
Brocade		X	X			X			Heavy silken fabric with raised design woven in
Cashmere	X	X				X	X		Very soft and fluid
Challis	X	X				X			Soft, lightweight, printed with floral patterns
Chenille		X		X				X	Apt to be super-fluffy yarn, tends to be quite bulky
Chiffon	X	X				X			Floaty and filmy
Corduroy		X	X	X			X	X	Has vertical ribbing; pinwale has less pile (bulk) than wide wale
Cotton									
Duck, Canvas, Sailcloth		X	X					X	Stiff and heavy, but strong
Combed Cotton, Pima, Liberty-style Italian Cotton	X					X	X	X	Soft, lightweight, and long-lasting
Denim		X	X					X	Comes in different weights; don't choose one too heavy for garment
Down		X		X				X	Amount of bulk depends on percentage of feathers to down; wear it to be warm, not tall
Felt		X	X					X	Very stiff, tends to stick out; for a fifties costume only
Fisherman Knit		X		X				X	Luscious and warm, but thick wool
Flannel		X	X					X	Tends to soften after laundering; plaid flannel requires extra caution
Lace	X					X			More expensive lace is softer
Leather/Suede	X						X	X	Choose soft, supple, higher-priced garments
Linen									
Handkerchief	X	X				X	X		Lightweight, soft
Homespun type			X				X	X	Coarse; more suitable for jacket

Fabric	PROBLEMS FOR PETITES					OVERALL LOOK			Comments
	Good for Petites	Wear with Caution	Stiff	Bulky	Reflects light	Feminine	Tailored	Casual	
Knits									
Wool, Jersey	X					X	X		Tend to drape nicely; don't wear too tight
Cotton	X						X	X	Comfortable and very wearable
Polyester		X							Not recommended for woman of any size; carries negative stigma
Mohair		X		X		X	X	X	Fluffiness creates bulk
Quilted Fabric		X	X	X				X	Fiberfill adds bulk and stiffness
Rayon	X					X	X		Can be made to look like cotton, crepe, wool; usually very fluid
Satin		X	X		X	X	X		For the thin petite only
Silk									
Broadcloth, Crepe de Chine	X					X	X		Lightweight; good for blouses or dresses
Shantung, Silk Linen	X					X	X		Nubby surface with slubs; especially for dresses, suits
Silk Taffeta, Velvet, Brocade		X	X			X	X		Luxurious but stiff
Taffeta		X	X			X	X		Reflects light, often stiff
Terry Cloth		X		X				X	Comfortable and absorbent, but bulky
Velour		X		X	X	X		X	Plush; best for petites with trim figures
Velvet		X		X	X	X	X		Makes objects look wider, not taller
Velveteen	X					X	X		Less pile, more lightweight than velvet
Woolens									
Gabardine, Challis, Crepe	X					X	X		Tightly woven, smooth fabric
Shetland, Pendleton-style Tweed		X	X	X			X	X	High quality, but of a bulky yarn

✳ Solid/print: Spark a solid-colored, flat-textured suit with a print scarf, rather than another solid.

✳ Texture/smoothness: The texture of a lace dress calls for smooth, unpatterned hose (in the same hue of course, to give you a flattering line). The rough texture of a novelty knit sweater—cables, popcorn stitch, or appliqué—needs smooth flannel or gabardine pants for balance.

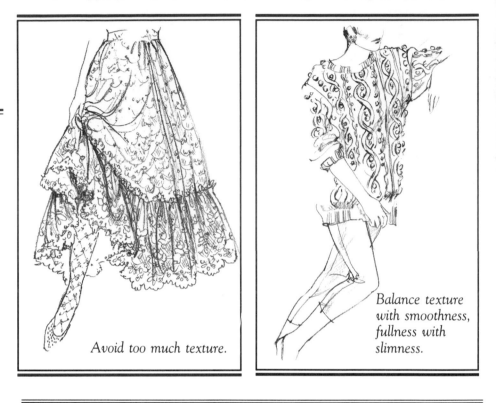

Avoid too much texture.

Balance texture with smoothness, fullness with slimness.

WOMEN TO LOOK UP TO

One of America's best-known entertainment reporters and CEO of her own communications company, **Rona Barrett** has interviewed the rich and famous for over twenty-five years. She has been a newspaper columnist, author, magazine editor, and television reporter/commentator. Her *Entertainment Report* is heard on over two hundred radio stations daily.

"I think BIG!" she says. "All my life I dreamed of who or what I was going to be or become. Most of the dreams became realities."

At 5'1", Ms. Barrett prefers clothes with classic lines and high fashion designs. She says with characteristic candor, "A long time ago I realized everything's an attitude. If you take yourself seriously and present your material in the same manner, height has nothing to do with anything—except for narrow-minded men who prefer having long-legged, flat-chested women as arm pieces, while most of these women yearn to be petite and more full-bodied! Ah, such is life!"

Your Longitude Quotient

Longitude is the foundation for petite-flattering looks. In this chapter you learned many ways to create it by using just three fashion concepts—line, proportion, and balance. To determine your L.Q. (Longitude Quotient), ask yourself the following questions when you check an outfit standing before your full-length mirror. Be aware that you don't have to answer yes to all of these questions. This checklist will help you achieve maximum longitude. But sometimes we want to give up a slight amount of longitude to gain fashion flair. In the next chapter, I'll show you how to do it and keep your L.Q. high.

Have I created a long line?

✳ Does my outfit have dominant vertical lines?

✳ Have I enhanced line with color? Am I wearing similar colors on my upper and lower torso?

✳ Does my outfit have built-in vertical lines—seams, closings, pattern?

✳ Does the detailing of my outfit—trim, pleats—give me verticals?

✳ Do my accessories create a long line? Are my hose similar to my hem in tone?

Do I bring the eye up?

✳ Do I repeat an accent color throughout my silhouette?

✳ Do I have accessories and/or detailing at my shoulders and face?

Are my clothes in proportion?

✳ Do they fit me with sufficient ease—not too tight?

✳ If I'm wearing an oversized garment, is it properly scaled to my body? (Oversized should not be overwhelming.)

✳ Are prints/plaids no larger than my hand?

✳ Do solid colors complement the print/plaid I'm wearing?

✳ Does the fabric flatter my figure? (It should not be too thick, stiff, or voluminous.)

Do the elements of my total outfit balance one another?

✳ Have I balanced clothes on top by those I'm wearing on the lower torso—full with form-fitting; long with short?

✳ Have I selected components (clothing, accessories) that push/pull—subdued/bright, solid/print, smooth/textured?

As you've become familiar with longitude, I suspect you've begun to evaluate clothes differently, both your own wardrobe and fashions you see at work, at restaurants, and on the street. Are you beginning to take note of line, proportion, and balance when you spot stylish looks on other petites? Do you notice ensembles (your own and others') that give the wearer longitude?

We'll continue to build on the basics as we apply our knowledge to some of the most-often-repeated rules for petite dressing. I think you'll understand how some rules came about, based on the concepts of line, proportion, and balance. And I know you're going to enjoy finding out how you can bend (and yes, even break!) rules to add your own flair.

Petite Style

CHAPTER 2

The Rules and How to Break Them

If you're like me, you've been inundated with rules for petite dressing. Mandates like "Always wear this" and "Never wear these" can quickly take the fun and excitement out of fashion. Although the rules were intended to help guide petites toward the most flattering looks, they have become overly rigid, stifling, and contrary to the image we want to create—that of a commanding, exciting, *stylish* woman.

I love it when I wear a paisley challis shawl over the shoulders of a fitted navy jacket and someone says admiringly, "I thought petites weren't supposed to wear big scarves. But that looks *gorgeous* on you!" Yes, petite woman *can* wear big scarves and a lot of other things we've been told not to wear. I'm going to show you how to do it—and I'm going to put the excitement back into dressing for you.

Unlike the three fashion principles you mastered in the last chapter, the list of rules is long. *Do not memorize them!* You know all you need to know about line, proportion, and balance. Now you'll learn precisely how to use those principles to disarm even the strictest rule and look totally marvelous. Fashions change—and there's always some new rule-breaking style to evaluate. So I'm also going to share with you six surefire techniques that will allow you to make a fashion statement by breaking the rules, not just based on today's fashions, but forever . . . my "Six Secrets to Lifelong Style."

BREAK THE RULES
WITH PETITE STYLE

Horizontal stripes . . . bright colors . . . cuffed pants . . . big, exotic prints . . . calf-length skirts. They've all been no-nos for petites. Until now.

The petite woman can wear virtually anything and look wonderful. The key is knowledge of longitude. As you will recognize in each example that follows, every time we break a rule, we're selecting other components of the outfit to create a long line, enhance proportion, and balance the rule-breaking item. The result: Petite flattery . . . *and* Petite Style.

Rule: Never Wear Horizontal Stripes

HOW TO BREAK IT

This is Rule Number One that many petites hear! There's no question that lively, fun horizontal stripes present a marked horizontal line. That's why, to break this rule with style, you need to pay attention to *what* kinds of horizontal stripes you wear and *where* they occur in an outfit. Some of my favorite clothes are striped, but they're narrow stripes, in subtle colorings, like lavender and cream, or soft gray, ivory, and fawn. As you can see in the illustrations, wide stripes produce an overpowering horizontal, whereas narrow stripes create a more flattering effect for petites. You won't go wrong with horizontals if you:

Bold horizontal stripes overpower the petite.   *Choose stripes that are narrow and subtle.*

* Look for horizontal stripes that create the illusion of a continuous line of color. Choose stripes in low-contrast colors, such as heather/blue/gray, rather than high-contrasts, such as green/yellow/red.

* Select narrow and irregular stripes. A pattern of mixed half- and one-inch stripes looks better than stripes that are all three inches wide, for example.

* Wear stripes where you can afford to look the widest: at the shoulders, or at the bust if you are small-busted.

* Wear a dress with a horizontal band of color around the hips *only* if you are very slim through the torso. Then balance it with heels and hose matched to your hem, and a long necklace or scarf to emphasize the vertical line.

* Belts are another horizontal, but I have a wonderful wide brown belt that I enjoy wearing with a suede dress plus another all-important piece—a long sleeveless coat in a luscious, nubby fabric, for a dominant vertical line.

Rule: Wear Only One Color

HOW TO BREAK IT

Color is one of the things I love about fashion. I love all colors—and I hate to stop with wearing just one. As we saw in Chapter 1, there are several ways to wear contrasting colors and maintain a long, flattering line:

* Wear colors of the same intensity, such as a purple skirt and navy blouse, or a mint green skirt and peach jacket.

* Wear a blouse in a contrasting color under a jacket or cardigan of the same color as your skirt or trousers.

* Wear your different color in accessories, carrying the color from top to toe in earrings, necklace, scarf, bracelet, or shoes.

Rule: Wearing Only Dark Colors

HOW TO BREAK IT

This rule evolved from two premises: (1) Dark colors will make you appear thinner, giving you a longer overall line. (2) Dark colors look more authoritative. Now, wearing dark colors is certainly not bad advice, but you surely don't have to limit yourself to them. The woman with Petite Style has many tricks for projecting an authoritative presence.

Just consider Rhea (5'). An artist, Rhea adores bright colors because they energize her. She looks smashing in her favorite fuchsia and yellow outfit that includes (top to toe) fuchsia earrings, a yellow tank under a fuchsia jumpsuit, yellow hose, and bright fuchsia shoes. Rhea *commands* attention when she enters a room in this vibrant combo . . . because she:

✳ Creates a continuous line of color. The dominant item in Rhea's ensemble, the jumpsuit, gives her a single vertical line.

✳ Brings the eye up with her bright yellow tank and fuchsia earrings.

✳ Employs the principle of balance to enhance longitude. Rhea's fuchsia and yellow are equally vibrant, so the intensity of color stays the same.

WOMEN TO LOOK UP TO

When actress **Cheryl Ladd** (5′4″) wants to get serious with her 6′2″ husband, "I make him sit down," she says. She relies on high heels and shoulder pads when they go out. With a slim figure (kept in shape by working out, riding, and rowing machines), Cheryl will wear anything, as long as it's in proportion. "That means it all has to move vertically: long sweaters, hipbone-length jackets, light tops with dark bottoms."

Rule: Never Wear Black and White

HOW TO BREAK IT

How can petites wear black and white? Creatively! The secret is to *avoid solid blocks* of these high-contrast colors. Choose a stunning black-and-white print, plaid, or combo. Accent it with smart black-and-white spectator shoes. I get endless compliments when I wear my long black-and-white houndstooth coat over a red wool jersey dress with a matching muffler. I could have sold that coat off my back many times!

Rule: Never Wear Cuffs on Trousers

HOW TO BREAK IT

Cuffs are best worn by a long-legged petite, because they do present a horizontal line. If you like the look of cuffed trousers, compensate for the horizontal:

✳ With a fit that skims the body.

✳ By wearing a top or jacket in a similar color.

✳ By choosing hose and shoes to match the pants.

Rule: Never Wear Big Prints

HOW TO BREAK IT

Proportion is critical here. The larger the print, the more you want to maximize longitude via other elements of your outfit. I do recommend, as in Chapter 1, that you keep the size of the print no larger than your hand. But that gives you a lot of room to play.

✳ Give yourself a vertical line by choosing a fabric that drapes and suggests the outline of your body.

✳ Choose a print in muted, low-contrast colors.

✳ Select a garment large enough to handle the print. A big print often works better on the volume provided by a dress than on a scarf or blouse.

✳ Bring the eye up by picking up a bright color of the print in your earrings.

Rule: Never, Never Mix Prints

HOW TO BREAK IT

Any petite can mix prints. The result will range from high-fashion to conservative, and it will always look distinctive. There is a wide range of prints available. Consider any of the following: herringbones, houndstooth checks, foulards, abstract geometrics, florals, paisleys, plaids. Mixing prints *does* require a sensitivity to line, proportion, and balance. It takes a practiced eye and a light touch.

✳ Mix darks with darks, lights with lights, brights with brights. That is, keep the colors in the different prints of a similar intensity.

✳ Balance the scale of the prints. You want them dissimilar enough to look interesting, yet no one print should overpower the others. Your petite body is too small to be a battleground!

✳ For best results, limit the number of prints you mix in any one outfit. Choose no more than three—and stick to subtle colorations.

✳ Mix identical prints done in two sizes, such as a miniprint (the size of quarters) with a micro-mini (the same print the size of dimes).

If you are new at print-mixing, start with any of the following to guarantee success: prints from manufacturers' lines that offer coordinated separates; prints all in one color family, such as a beige-and-white plaid with a beige-and-white paisley; positive/negative print combinations, such as red-on-blue print and the same design in blue-on-red.

The choices and combinations are endless . .. and full of flair.

Rule: Stick to Small Pieces of Jewelry

HOW TO BREAK IT

Be sure to break this rule! Accessories are so important to the petite that I've devoted the entire next chapter to them. For now, keep proportion in mind: Your jewelry should be in proportion to your body in the number of pieces and in the scale of each piece. This does *not* mean you have to wear the tiniest pieces available. Make them significant! In the next chapter you'll find specific guidelines for this fun element of Petite Style

Rule: Never Wear Oversized Clothing

HOW TO BREAK IT

Oversized is fine when it isn't overwhelming. Toni (4'11") tells me she prefers oversized styling because it helps her expand her physical space and exert more influence. I can testify that the result is dynamite—Toni always looks stylish. Follow these tips to maintain longitude:

❉ Balance the fullness of a blousy top/jacket on your upper torso by wearing form-fitting clothes, such as a slender skirt or tapered pants, on your lower torso.

❉ Give yourself a vertical by choosing hose and shoes to match your skirt and pants.

❉ Be superattentive to proportion if your big top is patterned. Since you're breaking a rule by going oversized, be sure you choose a print no bigger than your hand.

Rule: Never Wear Pleated or Gathered Skirts

HOW TO BREAK IT

I enjoy swingy skirts, but I look for those that fit closely through the tummy and hip, then flair out around the knees. It's the best of both worlds—fullness with no bulk around the middle. Excess fabric or thickness in a garment *can* throw you out of proportion and diminish longitude. To avoid this:

❉ Choose a skirt in a soft fabric for less bulk.

❉ Look for pleats that are stitched down across your tummy.

❉ Go for subtle colorations if the fabric is a print or plaid.

❉ Balance the fullness with body-skimming clothes on your upper torso.

❉ Be aware that pleated or gathered skirts are best worn by slender petites.

Rule: Wear Skirts No Longer Than Just Below the Knee

HOW TO BREAK IT

In spite of what you may have heard, petites do not have to wear any one skirt length. To determine the best length for you—and for an individual skirt—consult your full-length mirror. Try on the skirt with the shoes and a top you would expect to be wearing, so you can check your reflection for a long line and a balanced silhouette. Slowly slide the skirt up at the hips (or roll it at the waist) to get an idea of how much leg to reveal for the best overall look. Consider the style and shape of the skirt and the shape of your legs. For the most flattering leg look, don't end a skirt at the widest point of your calf.

Wear a *longer* skirt if:

✳ You are lucky enough to be proportionately long-legged.

✳ The fabric is not too heavy, nor is there so much fabric that it will drag you down.

✳ The skirt is cut on the bias and drapes the body nicely.

✳ You will be wearing boots that reach the hemline, to create a smooth line with skirt/boot.

Wear a *shorter* skirt if:

✳ You plan to wear hose in a similar hue to continue the line of color.

✳ The skirt is part of a conservative business look.

✳ You'll be wearing a higher heel.

✳ It feels best on you.

Whatever length you decide on, do make the necessary alterations—either shortening or lengthening. If you want your skirt *this* length, alter it. Just half an inch can make all the difference in how you look and feel . . . and how much you wear the skirt.

Rule: Always Match Your Hose to Your Shoes

HOW TO BREAK IT

Not only *can* you break this rule, you *should* break it much of the time. Visualize a black dress with burgundy shoes: Add burgundy hose and you'll create a choppy effect, whereas charcoal hose continue the line of the torso, for much more longitude. In the next chapter, on accessories, I'll give you detailed guidelines for selecting flattering hose to extend a long line.

WOMEN TO LOOK UP TO

"I think you develop a style of your own as you mature and have a better knowledge of yourself," states **Nancy Reagan.** Certainly the 5′4″, 105-pound First Lady has a unique presence and grace that are admired worldwide. Her impeccable sense of fashion has focused attention on her favorite American-based designers: Bill Blass, Adolfo, Oscar de La Renta, and Galanos.

"I think that so much of what is described as beauty comes from within," says Mrs. Reagan. "It's a sparkle that surfaces when a person is really happy with herself and feeling good about life. . . . I guess the most important advice I can give is to be the very best you can be in whatever you choose to do."

SIX SECRETS FOR LIFELONG STYLE

As my chic friend Robbi (5'3") comments, "When you break a rule, you add your own flair." Now you know how to break all of the most common rules and look great. But how do you decide to wear a daring look in the future? As fashions come and go, there will always be a new color scheme, a new style, a new way of wearing something that requires you to decide whether it is right for you. You can! You can artfully evaluate new fashions by applying what you've learned about longitude . . . by knowing how to break the most common rules . . . and by vowing that you will adopt these six secrets to practice from now on, for everlasting style.

1. Train Your Eye

Become friends with your full-length mirror. Look in the mirror daily before going out, then close your eyes and keep that image in your mind. Rely on your head-to-toe appearance to determine how you look in various colors and styles. Be alert to line, proportion, and balance. See how some outfits give you maximum longitude and others require you to compensate for breaking rules. Notice your favorite things in the mirror. What do you particularly like about them? The color? The cut? Carry those pictures of yourself in your mind. Now, when you see a rule-breaking look that appeals to you, try it . . . in your mind's eye. Eventually you'll be able to visualize yourself in new styles and make them work for you.

2. Experiment with Rule-Breaking Looks

Next time you see a tempting new fashion and wonder if it could work for you, make that your cue to experiment. When you can't immediately visualize how you might look in a brighter color, a larger earring, or a different style skirt, try it on. Then look in a *full-length mirror* to get the overall effect before you say aye or nay. After all, it doesn't cost anything until you buy it. Drop in to your favorite store for just half an hour, at a time when it doesn't matter if you find something or not, and *play* with things you haven't worn before. You'll have fun, and you'll fine-tune your sense of style.

3. Learn from Other Petites

Study good examples of rule-breaking on other petite women. Why does it work for them? Could it work for you? Perhaps it's a big scarf, a lower heel, larger accessories. How does it affect their overall appearance? Does it need other wardrobe elements—for instance, does a lower heel need a certain skirt length? Pick out those components that would work for you. I always preferred knee-length skirts. But as I saw more and more petites breaking this rule by wearing longer skirts—and looking attractive and stylish—I finally gave it a try. I was delighted with the results. Now longer skirts occupy an important place in my wardrobe.

4. Listen Carefully

We've all had that wonderful experience where we try something a bit daring and people we see all the time—at work or in the neighborhood—deluge us with compliments. "What a fantastic outfit!" "You look so radiant in that sweater!" "Where did you get that blouse?" As you bask in the warm glow of praise, give some thought to what people are responding to. Did you wear brighter colors than usual? If people single out a special element of your outfit, what do they mention—your jacket? your shoes? an attention-getting pair of earrings? When you hear compliments, relish them, and draw on this valuable information as you continue to develop your style.

5. Keep Current

What's in vogue? How can you adapt new looks to your small frame? Look for the trends, not short-lived fads. Learn from fashion magazines, newspaper ads, and fashion shows. Check out the streets and the stores. Salesclerks in most department stores and boutiques not only see the latest merchandise, they also keep abreast of what's coming up. Look at colors, figure accents (waist, hip), accessories, makeup, hair. What will fit your petite body and your personality?

6. Carry It Off with Confidence

As your look becomes more individual, expect to attract attention—and enjoy it. For a fine example of this, I always think of Marie (5'), who dresses with considerable panache. Marie chooses colorful, kooky outfits, such as blue-and-white polka-dot pants and a matching top with pink shoes and accessories. She invariably receives compliments on her ensembles, whether she's attending an art opening or a function for her husband, a corporate attorney. (She tells me, grinning, that he holds his breath waiting to see what she's going to wear!) "When people are true to themselves and feel comfortable, they can pull it off," says this stylish petite.

You have now seen that the rules for petite dressing are exaggerated. You may have also noticed that many of them overemphasize just one small aspect of the petite woman's image. For example, we've been told not to wear big earrings or calf-length skirts. But one item of clothing is not going to make or break an outfit. Petite Style means creating a total image—considering your entire appearance from head to toe.

As you select a dress, jacket, shoes, jewelry, you strive for a *long line* composed of elements that are *balanced* and in *proportion* to your petite frame. But you can look great in something that reduces longitude, like an oversized jacket or a sweater with horizontal stripes . . .

because now you know how to choose other components of your *total* outfit to flatter you to the utmost.

To break the rules successfully, you need that knowledge of how to compensate for rule-breaking items. Stylish rule-breaking also involves skills—training your eye, experimenting, observing other stylish petites, listening to compliments, keeping current, and carrying off a distinctive look with confidence. All of these will become second nature as you incorporate more rule-breaking, individual looks into *your* wardrobe. You're well on your way to having Petite Style.

Petite Style

CHAPTER 3

The Petite's Best Friend—Accessories

When people travel, they often pick up a souvenir beach bag or postcards to remind them of their trip. My husband, Dick, likes T-shirts emblazoned with the name of wherever we've been.

As for me, I buy accessories. When I was seven or eight, my family traveled through the Blue Ridge Mountains, where cranberries are grown, and my mother bought me a pretty bracelet made of glass beads the color and shape of cranberries. Wearing the bracelet brought back all the good memories of that vacation and gave me a lifelong penchant for commemorating journeys with accessories. Now my collection includes earrings from San Francisco, a purse from Georgia, and as mementos of Paris, earrings, a purse, *and* a scarf.

From my most sophisticated black hat to my favorite kicky tropical shoes, I love to discover how accessories can transform an outfit. Accessories create mood and excitement. Accessories allow you to diversify your wardrobe. More than any other fashion element, accessories help you create presence, personality, and panache.

As you'll see in this chapter, with just a few pieces you can:

✳ *Bring the eye up.* Rely on earrings, a necklace, a hat, or a scarf to focus attention on your face.

✳ *Enhance a long line.* Lengthen your visual image with hose and shoes that match your outfit.

✳ *Accentuate your figure assets.* Belt a tiny waist.

37

✳ *Pull an outfit together.* Unite separates by wearing a scarf or jewelry that incorporates their colors.

✳ *Create an impact.* Drape a shawl over one shoulder.

✳ *Project your personality.* Introduce a touch of whimsy with a rhinestone-studded lizard pin on your lapel.

No wonder I call accessories the petite's best friend. Let's begin your friendship with accessories by looking at the many different types of accessories. Then you'll find out how and when to accessorize to create your own Petite Style.

FROM TOP TO TOE

Let me share a secret about accessories that seems to give the women attending my seminars greatest pleasure—and creates the strongest fashion statement: *Wear significant earrings.* Earrings catch attention and enhance eye contact . . . especially when you choose at least a medium size. Petites are often told to stick to the smallest accessories, but I consider earrings the size of a quarter to be "medium" and recommend going even larger, depending on your outfit and the occasion.

As you select a pair of earrings (if you can stop at a single pair), experiment and try on the larger sizes. Then stand back from the mirror and appreciate the overall effect. Now, consider these questions before you buy:

✳ What will you wear them with? It's a special, entertaining challenge to find earrings that echo the colors or shapes in your clothes, such as an oversized "comma" shape in silver to repeat the shapes in your paisley skirt, ivory/ebony earrings to go with a black-and-ivory patterned sweater, or red disks edged in gold to echo the buttons in your navy jacket.

✳ Are they in proportion to your collar? You'll need shorter earrings to wear with a stand-up collar, a ruffled neckline, or a turtleneck.

Bring the eye up . . .

wear significant earrings.

✳ Do the earrings look good with your eyeglass frames? While plain frames that aren't overly large or prominent will permit you the greatest latitude in earring selection, don't feel you can't wear earrings because of your glasses. With all the earring styles available, you'll be able to find styles that go with any eyeglass frames. (By the way, don't overlook your glasses as an accessory item. You might want to have more than one pair—one neutral, another in your favorite color, and a third for evening.)

✳ Do the earrings complement the shape of your face? I like an oval or elongated earring because it balances my round face. A narrow, rectangular face looks best with the fullness of a wider, rounder earring.

✳ Will they work with your hairstyle? Earrings look particularly wonderful with short hair. If your hair usually covers your ears, consider wearing it differently to reveal a gorgeous pair of earrings.

Professional models always carry two or three pairs of classic earrings that will go with almost any fashion. Consider following their example and buying a few versatile basics, such as dime-sized pearls surrounded by gold, shiny gold disks, or gold hoops.

Beyond the basics, choose whatever earrings suit your fancy. The possibilities are limitless.

HATS

All accessories are important for the petite, but those worn close to the face are especially so, because they draw the eye up and give *you* longitude. Therefore, it's a good idea to wear a hat whenever it pleases your fancy. Less daring petites and others will notice and envy you. Choose a small black velvet chapeau with a veil for flirtatious evenings, a jaunty beret for weekends, or a brimmed wool felt with your favorite suit. (For a singular look that harks back to the forties, add a pair of gloves.)

I get compliments whenever I wear a hat. Once I was sitting at a restaurant and a handsome man—a total stranger—walked across the room and told me I looked great! This was no pickup, just a sincere compliment. Now that's hat-power!

When you're purchasing a hat, try on several to determine the right fit in the circumference and the best style for your face shape.

✳ Choose a hat in proportion to your petite size; one not too deep in the crown will look best on you.

✳ In the interest of proportion, look for a brim no wider than your shoulders.

✳ Experiment in the store: Try wearing the hat at different angles. Adjust the brim up or down. Add a jeweled pin at one side.

A wide hat brim overwhelms a petite woman.

Besides using the small mirror on the hat counter, look at your reflection in a full-length mirror to evaluate the overall effect. Ask yourself:

✳ Does this hat balance my outfit?

✳ Depending on what it's being worn with, is it simple or dressy enough?

✳ Is the hat color repeated elsewhere in the outfit?

✳ Does it echo the mood of the outfit?

Incidentally, if you have trouble finding a summer straw hat that fits tightly enough to stay on your head in a breeze, try securing it with a hatpin. They really do work.

WOMEN TO LOOK UP TO

"When I consider a garment, I think, 'Does this make me look like I make $250,000 a year?' If the answer is no, I don't buy it," says **Patricia Fripp.** Ms. Fripp, 5′1″, came to America from Britain at age twenty with only five hundred dollars in her pocket. She is now a motivational speaker who is in demand all over the country. Patricia Fripp relishes vivid colors and her trademark, *big* hats.

"Develop your own style and don't be afraid to make an impact," she says.

Choose a hat in proportion to your size, with a brim that is narrower than your shoulders.

SCARVES

I treasure accessories I've received as gifts. For example, friends of my parents gave me a beautiful white scarf with splashes of teal blue for my high school graduation. It was of fine quality and I kept it, even though I never had an outfit that really set it off. This year (during which I happened to celebrate my twenty-first high school reunion!) I bought a white two-piece knit dress and a teal sweater-coat. It's an elegant ensemble . . . and the scarf is the *pièce de résistance!*

Scarves are wondrously versatile and should be a staple in every petite's accessory collection. The artist's bow that became popular with the preppy look is only one of the many exciting possibilities. You can also wear scarves in the form of oversized paisley squares, silk bias ties, silk pocket squares, lamé oblongs, mufflers, and gauze waist wraps.

Trust me—scarf-tying is *not* difficult. You can adapt a few basic tying techniques to scarves worn around the head, neck, or waist, and to scarves of different fabrics. For example, the classic bow takes on a different look entirely done with a soft oblong, a crisp oblong, or a narrow bias scarf. See Appendix A for tips on scarf-tying.

Buying a Scarf

Scarves come in all shapes and sizes: big squares, pocket squares, oblongs, and biases. A long oblong or bias scarf gives you versatility; wear it at the waist, the neck, or around the crown of a hat. A square scarf can be folded into an oblong for more possibilities.

I prefer to buy scarves made of soft, lightweight fabrics such as silk, gauze, fluid jersey, chiffon, and loose weaves, which can be draped, pleated, and knotted with a minimum of bulk. I always unfold the scarf in the store, to see its effect as a whole. Questions to ask yourself when you're shopping for scarves include:

 ✳ Is the pattern scaled to the size of the scarf—and to me?

 ✳ What other colors appear at the center of the scarf?

 ✳ How can the shape of the scarf best enhance a particular piece of clothing?

Wearing a Scarf

When you wear a scarf, you don't want to have to fuss with it constantly. Anchor it invisibly with a safety pin . . . or use a beautiful brooch that deserves to be seen. (Just be sure not to create a pucker in the fabric.) Here are some more tips on enhancing your image with scarves:

 ✳ Use a scarf to bring out a color in your outfit or to unite the colors of your separates—like my white-and-turquoise scarf with my white dress/teal coat combination.

✳ Draw attention and save money by letting a scarf do double duty. Wear it in place of a hat, necklace, or belt.

✳ Enhance a vertical line by using a scarf as a shawl draped over one shoulder, or an oblong hanging loosely under the lapels of your jacket.

✳ Drape a square scarf at the neck in place of a necklace.

Scarves lend drama.

NECKLACES

I always feel an unadorned expanse of bodice begs for a necklace. Depending on its length and style, a necklace can give you a great vertical line. The best necklace for a petite is generally twenty to thirty inches in length. (Necklaces are measured from end to end, excluding the clasp.) Of course you can go longer or shorter for style and personal preference.

For longitude and flair try:

✳ A long, thick rope necklace

✳ A significant pendant

✳ A "standard" strand of pearls anchored midway with a stunning pin

✳ Two or three strands of gold and pearls (à la Chanel)

Longer length necklaces add longitude and flair.

Chunky necklaces that fit close to the neck create a horizontal line, but worn with a plain jewel neckline, they can make a smashing fashion statement. Never, however, ruin a marvelous, long V-neckline with a choker.

If you like a long necklace, wear it . . . with these few exceptions. Avoid:

✳ Anything so long it swings against your desktop as you work

✳ A necklace that stops right at a full bosom

✳ Too long a necklace for a short-waisted figure (that is, a necklace that approaches your waist)

PINS AND BROOCHES

Small but mighty, pins and brooches can give a great finishing touch to an outfit. Pam (5′3″) told me she hadn't worn a pin since she was a teenager, but one day recently she was in a store trying on a cream silk broadcloth blouse; the blouse featured a high collar with overlapping points. Suddenly the saleswoman exclaimed, "I know what you need!" She dashed out of the fitting room and returned with an oblong gold pin with a pearl in the center that she placed at Pam's throat, joining the two sides of the collar. Pam can't imagine wearing the blouse without it now.

Take advantage of pins and brooches for both ornamental and functional wear.

✻ Use a lovely brooch to anchor a scarf or necklace for worry-free wear. (Do make sure the fabric doesn't pucker.)

✻ Use pins and brooches to add personality to a suit jacket, especially if your blouse is too busy for a necklace.

✻ Use pins and brooches as conversation starters. Think of the comments you'll elicit when you wear an exotic dragon pin crafted of silver with a ruby eye on your lapel, or a jeweled butterfly on your shoulder.

✻ Don't confine these great accessories to your shoulders. A favorite pin can spice up a simple hat or beret, and give you flair.

BRACELETS

Bracelets may present a challenge for petites. Many small-boned petites complain to me that bangle bracelets intended to slide on over the hand drop right off when they put down their arms. To fit a tiny wrist, shop for bracelets that are made small in circumference or have a clasp. You can also have watches or chain bracelets altered to fit. Small-wristed petites may do best with a cuff bracelet that grasps the arm two to three inches above the wrist.

When you find bangle bracelets that fit you, go for a significant wrist! Wear them in pairs . . . and don't limit yourself to the thinnest bands.

LEFT *Wear a pin for a finishing touch.*

RIGHT *Enjoy selecting and wearing bracelets that fit properly.*

BELTS

If your waist is tiny, flaunt it by wearing a significant belt! Go with a belt in a contrasting color to your outfit, a beaded belt, or one that otherwise calls attention to itself.

As for the rest of us, since belts do present a horizontal line, I advise choosing one in a color that blends with your outfit. You'll also counteract the horizontal by wearing the belt under a third layer like a jacket; the vertical line of the jacket edges will offset the belt's shortening effect. Some more belt tips:

✳ Use belts for figure flattery. You can wear a belt wrapped about your waist to rein in fullness through the torso and slim a wide silhouette. If you're short-waisted, wearing a belt low on your hips will help balance your proportions.

✳ Belts seldom come smaller than twenty-four inches, so be sure yours fits neatly. Have a shoe repair shop made an additional hole to make it smaller and either trim the excess on the end or tuck it underneath.

✳ Belts three-quarters of an inch to two inches wide are great for petites. To wear a wider belt, wrap it around your hips rather than your waist, and choose a color that blends with your outfit. Otherwise, you risk throwing your silhouette out of proportion. My pet peeve is the belt so wide it "catches" on my rib cage and fits like a corset. These should be marked "for long-waisted petites only."

Don't overlook the possibilities of scarves or strips of fabric fashioned as belts. See Appendix A, "Scarf-Tying Techniques."

LEFT *Belts give figure flattery.*

PURSES

Thank heaven purses no longer have to match shoes. We now have many more creative possibilities. Nevertheless, do coordinate your purse with your outfit for a put-together look *and* greater longitude. The purse you carry appears as part of your overall silhouette, so follow these tips to ensure balance and proportion:

✳ Carry the smallest bag that will accommodate your needs. Size is an important factor for petite women. When I need a lot of room, I select a bag that is large but flat—it should hang close to my body or fit under my arm—rather than a smaller bag that is bulky and cumbersome.

✳ Don't overload your small frame. Don't carry a large handbag *and* a briefcase or tote. Consider a bag within a bag: a small one for your personal essentials carried inside a tote or briefcase. I like to carry the small bag, with just what I need for a lunch or a meeting, and leave my carry-all in the trunk of my car.

✳ Look for handbags made of soft, flexible leather, vinyl, or fabric. They will look less bulky than bags made of hard or stiff materials.

✳ Styles that are especially becoming include: the clutch, envelope, and quilted Chanel bags with chain handles. These are thin, without gussets to add bulk. Avoid bulky styles such as duffle sacks, buckets, doctors' satchels, and hobos.

A bulky purse disrupts your total silhouette.

Choose a flat purse that hangs close to the body.

＊ For easy access, shoulder bags should not extend below your hand. If necessary, have the chain or strap adjusted by a shoe repair shop. If the strap is very thin, narrow leather, you may simply tie a knot in it.

＊ *Do* be kind to your appearance and your back! Don't add bulk with what you put *in* your purse.

HOSIERY

Hosiery plays an important role in enhancing longitude. In general, match your stockings to your skirt or trousers to continue one long line of color. In other words, wear ivory hose with a winter-white skirt, charcoal or off-black with a black skirt, pale peach hose with peach. With a skirt in an intense color, however, balance the vividness with neutral hose. In Claire's makeover in Chapter 9, she wears a red ensemble with gray accents and gains longitude with pearly-gray hose.

Remember the technique of bringing the eye up for longitude: You want brighter color around your shoulders and face than on your legs. Thus, you should keep the color of your legs muted in comparison to the color of your clothes. Choose ultra-sheer stockings for a tint of color, rather than boldly colored hose. If you wear sheer stockings with patterns, keep them subtle. Wear them only if you consider your legs an asset, because they *will* draw attention. Opaque and textured stockings should be reserved for slender legs—and only with longer skirts and heavier, low-heeled shoes for nondressy occasions.

Anklets have become popular in recent years. Personally, I don't like them on petites for two reasons: They create a little-girl look, and they "chop up" your image. If you do want to wear anklets, be sure to balance the rest of your outfit for maximum longitude. Anklets are best worn by petites with long, slender legs.

Now that you are aware of hosiery guidelines and why they work for petites, you can decide for yourself when to bend a rule in favor of fashion. For example, if black is a popular clothing color for the season, worn with a sheer, pale leg, I may choose to follow suit, knowing that what I lose in a long leg, I gain by being in the forefront of fashion.

SHOES

Finally we come to the foot of the matter—many petites' favorite place. Women with petite feet can wear a wide selection of shoes with confidence . . . and with the envy of their larger-footed sisters. Do you love shoes? Indulge yourself with classic spectators, the look of exotic snake or alligator pumps, fringed boots, skimmers in iridescent brights, loafers with chain detailing. You have a myriad of possibilities!

Shoe Style

The most flattering shoe styles for the petite are those that make your legs look longer. Look for shoes with a long throat and a V-shaped, rather than rounded, vamp (the top edge of the shoe). Closed toes

Especially becoming styles are the clutch and the envelope.

also give you a long, flattering line. Use the same principle to determine what styles to avoid. Shoes with straps or lacing around the ankle create horizontal lines that may make your leg look stubby. Open-toed shoes and sandals can make your foot appear shorter and wider.

Keep your shoes in proportion to your legs. Exceptionally thin legs look best in delicate shoes and not-too-high heels; very high heels may make them appear spindly. Heavy legs look best in a substantial shoe.

Virtually any style boot will elongate your image. Make sure it reaches your hem, to avoid the choppy effect of skirt/leg/boot. Another long look comes from tucking your pant leg into your boot.

Wear boots that elongate your image.

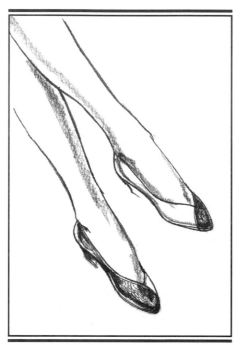

LEFT *Choose shoes that extend a long leg line.*

BELOW *Avoid shoes with horizontal lines.*

To Heel or Not to Heel

Many petite women enjoy the psychological lift of wearing high heels. Heels look terrific on petites; they make legs look longer and add height and elegance. But don't make the mistake of thinking the higher the heel the better. Three- to four-inch heels throw a small woman out of proportion and her back out of alignment. Besides, at a time when flat and almost-flat shoes are considered high fashion, many petites are eagerly accepting that look.

I was one of those who once wouldn't buy tennis shoes unless they were high-heeled sneakers! But I kept seeing such tempting flat shoes. At last I was seduced by a pair of dark brown flats with exquisite workmanship. Done in snakeskin, they featured piping in a lighter shade of brown and lacing in top. I bought them to wear with a pair of dark brown leather pants. Those luscious shoes convinced me that flat and low-heeled shoes have a place in my wardrobe. My latest acquisition? A one-inch heel in bright tropical colors, perfect for sipping margaritas poolside.

If you're reluctant to hang up your high heels for good, try a lower-heeled shoe for casual wear, with longer skirts, when you're not under pressure to make an imposing entrance. You'll be pleasantly surprised to find how flattering low heels can be. You'll reap a health benefit as well. Wearing high heels over many years shortens your calf muscles; by alternating between higher and lower heels, you'll restore important flexibility to your legs. Our spines are also happier when we wear lower-heeled shoes.

LEFT *Indulge a shoe fancy.*

WOMEN TO LOOK UP TO

5'4" singer **Melissa Manchester** has three-inch heels specially designed so she can indulge her passion for "killer high heels" on stage without sacrificing comfort. When performing and at home, she likes to wear lots of accessories and makeup. For business meetings, she prefers classic designer clothes. A Grammy Award-winner, Melissa says, "I just sing tall."

Small Feet, Large Feet

If you're a petite with equally petite feet, you may have trouble finding shoes in your size. In general, the smaller your foot, the harder it is to find shoes that fit, so shop early in the season. I've also discovered a number of stores that cater to small-footed women and offer shoes by mail order. These stores are listed in the "Petite Shopper's Directory" in the Appendix.

If, however, your feet are proportionately large, there are several ways to create balance:

✳ Wear shoes in darker shades.

✳ Make an effort to coordinate hem, hose, and shoes.

✳ Avoid platform shoes and bulky styles with thick heels.

Footwear and Longitude

What happens when we don the most wonderful, stylish shoes in every color of the rainbow? We glance down as we're walking, just to admire those bright new pumps or boots . . . and so does everyone else. But you don't have to give up longitude when you wear eye-catching shoes, as long as you consider these options:

✳ Match your shoes to your hem and hose; you'll still maintain a long line.

✳ Wear shoes in a contrasting color, then achieve balance by repeating the color throughout your silhouette. Echo your favorite yellow pumps in a yellow bangle bracelet and yellow scarf, and you'll gain longitude and Petite Style.

THE HOW OF ACCESSORIES

We all know the story of Goldilocks and the Three Bears. Stumbling into the bears' house, Goldilocks tried all three bowls of porridge, all three chairs, and all three beds. Each time, she rejected the extremes ("too hot," "too cold"), until she found the one that was "just right."

We want to strive for the same "just rightness" with accessories. Jewelry, belts, hose, shoes, hats, and scarves are the primary source of interest in an outfit. Too little interest, and the outfit's drab. Too much, and it's overdone. The following checklist will help you determine when you have just the right amount of interest in an outfit. Give yourself a point for each element of interest, and aim for four to seven points total.

Let's look at how three different women come out on the following test.

ACCESSORIES

Your Guideline to Looking Great

Strive for four to seven points.

YOUR CLOTHES

Jacket, shawl, vest, sweater, or coat	1 point
Plaid or patterned clothes	
Upper torso	1 point
Lower torso	1 point
Large blocks of contrasting colors	1 point
Significant detailing: braid, trim, ruffles, gold buttons, chain, beading, appliqué	1 point

YOUR ACCESSORIES

Significant Jewelry	
Earrings	1 point
Necklace	1 point
Bracelet	1 point
Pin or brooch	1 point
Scarf	1 point
Ornate or colored shoes/boots	1 point
Patterned or textured hose	1 point
Black or colored hose	1 point
Wide or contrasting belt	1 point
Hat	1 point
Hair ornament or bow	1 point
Ornate, colorful, or very large purse	1 point

If your total is—

1–3	Your outfit is too understated. Accessorize for more pizzazz.
4–7	You look just right. Your outfit has interest and impact, yet *you* wear your clothes—*they* don't wear *you.*
8 or more	Your outfit is overstated. Remove something so people don't lose sight of *you.*

Myra wears a matching camel suit and a pin-stripe blouse, with a silk tie at her neck. She adds small studs at her ears, a narrow belt, neutral hose, and plain pumps. She carries a small handbag. She gets one point for the jacket and one for the belt, for a total of two . . . and absolutely no impact. Neither the earrings nor the tie are significant enough to be counted. (See page 52)

Kathy goes all out in the other direction. She wears a black suit with detailing provided by big buttons on the jacket (one point for the jacket, one point for the detailing), a blouse with an overly large bow (one), and an attention-getting wide belt (one). She accessorizes with large drop earrings (one), a bracelet (one), gloves (one), black patterned stockings (one), and black shoes. She carries a box-like shiny black purse (one)—for a total of nine points. Kathy's personality is buried under all these fussy details. A little moderation, and *she* would shine through.(See page 52)

Kelly wears an ivory blouse and navy skirt, topped with a jacket (one point) in a subtle navy-and-burgundy tweed, sparked with a pocket handkerchief (one). She adds medium-sized silver earrings (one), a long necklace (one), and a link bracelet (one). Notice she doesn't go for the smallest jewelry, but chooses significant pieces. She carries an envelope handbag. To complete the outfit she wears hose with a hint of navy (one) and textured navy pumps (one). Her accessories enhance her clothes, her figure, and her personality . . . and at the same time you can see *her.* Kelly scores a seven on the Accessories Test—and a perfect 10 on Petite Style. (See page 52)

51

Petite Flair

LEFT *Apply the Accessories Test to prevent Myra's problem, a lack of interest . . .*

Petite Style

BELOW: *or too much—Kathy's problem.*

BELOW RIGHT *like Kelly, gain impact, with accessories that are "just right."*

THE WHEN OF ACCESSORIES

New accessory "must-haves" appear every spring and fall, and for holidays seasons. I like to listen to the forecast of the latest *colors* (black, salmon, teal), *materials* (anything silver, faux gems), and *styles* (multiple strands of pearls, head scarves worn Grace Kelly–style. Then I make up my own mind about which trends to follow.

Although trends change with changes in fashion, the *when* of accessories also has to do with seasons of the year and time of day. Evening dressing calls for jewelry that sparkles. I like to see relaxed, show-off-a-tan summer fashions accompanied by spare, easy accessories. Observe the following recurring themes and general guidelines to help you develop a basic wardrobe of timeless accessories; then add some of each season's "must-haves" when you're so inclined.

Daytime Accessories

SUMMER

Pastels often appear in spring. They're joined by brights and whites in summer. Among summer classics: nautical themes, spare, easy-fitting fashions; and natural fabrics that breathe—cotton, gauze, linen, and silk. Tropical and floral prints abound. Here are some specifics:

Jewelry:	Colored enamels, wood, natural materials like ebony, bone. However, gold or silver is always chic.
Shoes:	Sandals, espadrilles, open-toed.
Purses:	Canvas, straw, fabric.
Hose:	Sheer, pale colors.
Scarves:	Gauze, cotton, silk.
Hats:	Straw, fabric. Also headwraps.
Other:	Sunglasses can also make a statement as jewelry for the face. I consider them notable summer accessories.

Summer classics include nautical themes, spare, easy-fitting fashions, and natural fabrics that breathe.

WINTER

As autumn approaches, earth colors and animal prints often appear. With winter, look for darker colors, jewel tones, and winter white. Wool and silk are prevalent, sparked with tapestry, tweed, plaid, and paisley. Seasonal basics include:

Jewelry: Mostly metal—gold or silver. Pearls, gold chains, semi-precious stones.

Shoes: Closed-toe shoes; boots.

Purses: Lots of leather.

Hose: Sheer, opaque, or textured hose.

Scarves: Silk, wool, challis.

Hats: Wool, felt.

Other: Wool or leather gloves, to coordinate with coat or to match hat and muffler in bright contrasting color.

Evening (all year)

For nighttime, fashion favors sultry black or sophisticated white, as well as intense, glow-in-the-dark colors like cobalt blue, red, and magenta. Fabrics include silk, satin, velvet, or anything that incorporates metallic threads, sequins, or beads. Other components include:

Jewelry: Larger earrings, in drop styles. Hair ornaments. Choose something that glitters, like rhinestones, faux jewels—or the real thing.

Shoes: Cut-out styles, generally with a heel. Have fabric shoes dyed to match or select black satin, metallic gold, or silver. Add an ornamental clip along the edge.

Purses: Small, in leather, fabric, or beaded.

For winter, look for darker colors, jewel tones, and winter whites—in wool and silk.

Hose:	Patterned, often in blackened shades or with an iridescent tint.
Scarves:	For accent in hair, at neck, or at waist; also oversized scarves as shoulder wraps. Consider scarves with metallic thread, edged with maribou, or made of velvet, brocade.
Hats:	Small with veil, feathers, jewels.
Other:	Gloves—in black or white, reaching to the elbow.

Evening fashion favors sophistication in fabric and color.

Remember . . . you'll gain longitude when you wear accessories, especially around your head and shoulders. *Do* wear earrings, hats, necklaces, and scarves to bring the eye up to your highest point and direct attention to your face.

You will make an impact by wearing strong accessories. Choose just a few items—silver earrings, a leather belt, a silver cuff bracelet—and make them significant. You'll have fun wearing an earring or bracelet larger than you thought you could wear, and you'll gain style.

The simpler your outfit, the more it begs to be adorned and the more choice you'll have as to accessories. Accessorize solid colors, plain necklines, uninterrupted bodices, and simple styling. Remember the accessories test to strike a beautiful balance when you accessorize.

In the next chapter we'll be creating stunning new outfits out of what you already have in your closet. As you apply your knowledge of accessories, I think you'll agree with me that accessories are the petite's best friend!

CHAPTER 4

Wardrobe Arithmetic

By this time, you're using your knowledge of line, proportion, and balance to look your best. You've learned to break the rules to add your own flair. You understand how to make an impact with accessories. Now comes the fun of wardrobe arithmetic.

I'm going to show you how two plus two equals . . . six or seven or eight! Now, I never taught this unconventional addition to my first-graders, but as an image consultant, I have discovered that wardrobe arithmetic makes perfect sense. Each time I got to a woman's house, we begin to make new outfits—from what she already has in her closet. Two skirts plus two blouses combine to form the basis for at least half a dozen distinctive, stylish ensembles.

In this chapter, I'd like you to imagine I've come to *your* house to do an image consultation. Together we are going to discover the fantastic combinations hanging in your closet. I guarantee that we'll find more than you suspect. Once we have accomplished that, we'll set your shopping priorities.

First, let's sit down and discuss two concepts that I use every time I put together an ensemble: Attitude and the Rule of Three. You will gain versatility in your wardrobe, infuse your personal flair into outfits, and dress with polish and authority when you employ just these two basic concepts.

ATTITUDE

A classic strand of pearls, a lacy handkerchief, a peasant blouse, a man-tailored tweed blazer: Each has its own personality, what I call attitude. I'm sure you are already sensitive to the effect of attitude on mood (your own and others') and the importance of matching the attitude of your clothes to the situation. For instance, when you don your turquoise jacket with a palm tree appliqué to meet friends at a coffeehouse, the sense of fun in the jacket energizes you and everyone around you. But you'd never wear that jacket to a job interview at a bank.

Attitude does more than just create mood, however. Understanding the concept of attitude will help you adapt your wardrobe for business, casual, and dressy occasions. What's more, *you can use attitude creatively to diversify your wardrobe and make a fashion statement.* First let's look at the four basic attitudes: executive, feminine, casual, and eclectic. Then we'll talk about how you can use your knowledge of attitude to perform wardrobe arithmetic.

Of the four basic attitudes, one or two may describe most of your wardrobe, while a third might characterize a few special items . . . or the image you desire.

Casual Attitude

My favorite casual wear is sweaters. They feel so good! I like to wear a sweater with a pair of leather pants and flats when I'm entertaining friends. Clothes for the casual attitude, typified by a relaxed suburban or country mood, include unmatched separates and soft fabrics like corduroy and denim. Look for plaids, checks, tweeds, comfortable low-heeled shoes, and accessories made of natural materials such as wood and ivory; also Western wear, with its silver and turquoise jewelry.

Executive Attitude

When I want to project the ultimate in authority, I select most of my clothes from this category—crisp wool suits, tasteful gold earrings, and fine leather pumps, for example. Executive clothes range from menswear styling to softer looks, such as suits without lapels and classically tailored silk dresses. Colors associated with this attitude are darks and neutrals. Prints tend to be small geometrics. Rich fabrics such as silk, wool, and linen, and quietly elegant accessories also characterize the executive attitude.

Feminine Attitude

Romantic ruffles and lace come to mind. They reflect the feminine attitude, as do velvet, challis, Victorian jewelry, delicate sandals, pastels, and floral prints. Sometimes we reveal our femininity in a more sensual manner, as seen in off-the-shoulder blouses, seductive gowns à la Jean Harlow, sexy black, and provocative white. I like to use a touch of this attitude to soften my business wardrobe . . . and I go all-out feminine when I want to feel my most romantic. Candlelight dinners call for soft, touchable fabrics—and underneath them, sensuous lingerie.

59

Petite Flair

LEFT *Casual Attitude: for a relaxed, at-ease look.*

BELOW RIGHT *Feminine Attitude: from the romantic to the sensual.*

BELOW LEFT *Executive Attitude: for the ultimate in authority.*

Eclectic Attitude

This look may involve antique, ethnic, art deco, high-tech—you name it! "Creative types"—artists, boutique owners, and rock stars, for example—can wear high-energy eclectic clothes whenever they like. Many other petites dress eclectic only for evenings and weekends. As for me, I enjoy using a touch of this attitude—a funky pin, a bright jacket—to spice up an ensemble. Eclectic clothes are marked by vibrant color combinations, such as red and purple, or turquoise and yellow. Prints include large geometrics and distinctive motifs, such as fish, fruit, and human figures.

Eclectic Attitude: to express your creative side.

Attitude Plus Wardrobe Arithmetic Equals Style

Last year I designed a solid-periwinkle blue dress. I added detailing in the form of black mother-of-pearl buttons on shoulder epaulets and in back from the neck to the waist. I continued the black accent—and the executive attitude—by wearing the dress with a black hat, bag, shoes, and jewelry. All in all, this ensemble yields a quiet, sophisticated mood. But I don't want to be quietly sophisticated all the time! I purchased a fashionably bright yellow silk jacket that effectively—and eclectically—covers the black buttons on the dress. When I wear the blue dress/yellow jacket combo, I don dt low heels with a multicolored tropical flower pattern, a bright print scarf that includes the precise shade of the dress, and blue/yellow earrings. By going eclectic, I give the dress a totally different feeling—exciting and fun to wear.

Just as I turned one blue dress into two distinctive outfits, you can combine attitude and wardrobe arithmetic to discover new possibilities in your wardrobe and dress with Petite Style. You won't go wrong when you follow these guidelines.

MIX ATTITUDES TWO AT A TIME

Attitude mixing lets you expand your wardrobe and express your personality. The result will always be distinctive and stylish . . . as long as you stick to just two of the four attitudes in any one outfit. Liven up your executive suit with an eclectic parrot pin, or soften it with a feminine lace jabot; just don't do both at one time. Two attitudes look interesting and stylish. Three (or, heaven forbid, all four) give a discordant, confused, message. So by all means, top a casual denim skirt with a ruffled feminine blouse or petticoat to give it a romantic air. Choose feminine satin pants with a camisole and kimono in an eclectic color scheme to show off your softness *and* your sense of whimsy. As you become sensitive to the attitude of different garments, you'll instinctively practice this aspect of Petite Style.

TAKE ADVANTAGE OF "ATTITUDE CHAMELEONS" FOR VERSATILITY AND STYLE

While many garments broadcast their attitude loud and clear, some clothes have quieter personalities. Very simple garments, like a plain gray wool skirt or a round-necked cream-colored blouse, are "attitude chameleons," which makes them wonderful backgrounds against which your high-attitude clothes can dazzle. Using the same "chameleon" dress—a just-below-the-knee-length basic ivory with a plain neck and long sleeves—you can develop four different ensembles, each projecting a different *attitude*.

✳ To give the outfit an executive attitude, cinch the dress at the waist with a narrow gold chain. Don a white jacket trimmed with blue braid, a pearl necklace, and coin earrings. The final touches—pale hose with navy spectators.

✳ For a feminine attitude, accessorize the ivory dress with lace stockings, pale pink shoes, and a Victorian choker. Wear small hearts on your ears and carry an antique beaded bag.

✳ Make this dress casual with a loose tweed jacket, a leather belt at the hip, loafers, and a necklace of carved wooden beads.

✳ The dress can go eclectic as well, proving there's no rest for the wearable. Hike it up to tunic length with a belt, pull on patterned tights, pin a rhinestone-studded leopard on your shoulder, and top the outfit with a neon-bright beret.

By exploring all the possibilities presented by attitude chameleons, you'll double the potential of your wardrobe, for an equation that can't fail to produce Petite Style.

WOMEN TO LOOK UP TO

Harper's Bazaar named **Lisa Bonet** (5′2″) one of "America's 10 Most Beautiful Women" when she was just eighteen! The vivacious actress established a terrifically kooky—and always stylish—image as daughter Denise on *The Cosby Show*. But she says it's not her current look offscreen. "When I auditioned for the series, I was in my funky period," says Lisa. "Bill Cosby loved the effect—even the outrageous hats and jewelry. So that's why my character, Denise, continues to display an avant-garde image." Meanwhile, her private look has become more lacy and feminine. In 1987, Lisa sizzled in her first major film role, in *Angel Heart*.

THE RULE OF THREE

You've learned to recognize the four basic attitudes and seen how to mix two attitudes at a time for a distinctive look. What could come next in wardrobe arithmetic but that special number, *three*. From the three sides of a triangle to the three branches of U.S. government, the number three traditionally denotes a sense of completion and wholeness. It can do the same thing for your wardrobe.

You can turn any outfit into a more polished ensemble when you follow the Rule of Three: *Always wear at least three items for a finished look and a heightened image.*

Select your top and skirt or slacks, then choose the all-important third piece: a jacket, vest, sweater, or shawl. Adding a third layer on your upper torso turns ordinary separates into an ensemble. It gives you longitude by directing the eye to the top of your body and subtly broadening the line of your shoulders. It also lends you credibility: Betty Harragan in *Games Mother Never Taught You* calls a jacket "your mantle of authority." You can see how we applied this principle to Ruth's Tené's, and Claire's makeovers in Chapter 9.

The following tips will help you apply the Rule of Three as you go through your closet and plan outfits for specific occasions:

✳ For the *most* commanding effect, the third piece should be a jacket that matches your skirt. This also provides the most longitude, because the line of color continues from the top to bottom of the ensemble. Although clothing standards for women in business have relaxed in recent years, a matched suit is still at the top of my list for job interviews, boardrooms, presentations, and meeting clients for the first time. Depending on the situation, your options range from the most conservative of executive looks to softer, more feminine styling. Consider:

> Traditional menswear styling (structured with lapels)
> A softer jacket (no lapels, velvet collars)
> Wrap styles
> Long, sleek lengths
> Shorter lengths with flyaway backs
> A jacket nipped in at the waist with a peplum

✳ A matched suit carries the most authority, but you will also make an impact wearing a jacket over a tailored dress.

✳ To achieve a more casual but still polished look, choose a jacket that complements rather than matches your outfit, such as a bright blazer, a tweed hacking jacket, a pea jacket, or a jacket with a mandarin collar. Fabric, styling, and attitude choices abound.

✳ Make the Rule of Three go high-fashion by wearing a long coat or duster in natural silk or gabardine with either a skirt or trousers. This can be the essence of urban style!

✳ Knits are very comfortable to wear and range from elegant to relaxed. Choose one like the double-breasted sweater jacket that Tené wears in her makeover (4 color insert), a full-length sweater coat, or a Chanel-inspired knit cardigan with gold chain trim.

✳ A shawl, cape, or ruana carries power and polish when you enjoy a bit of drama. (You *can* wear these as long as they are proportionate to your size.) Depending on the climate, you can wear a shawl over the shoulders of a jacket or coat; it also counts as piece number three when worn alone. Choices range from soft paisley squares to fringed cashmere rectangles to loose, luscious textured weaves, for either a feminine or an eclectic attitude and lots of style.

✳ At the height of summer, when it is 95 degrees outside, you can still keep your cool and follow the Rule of Three. Choose a light-weight third layer, perhaps an unlined jacket. Or wear a third layer made from a natural fabric. Light colors are also cooler. Choose a third layer that fits loosely—nothing tight or binding. Remember, your third layer can be as little as a scarf. Finally, you can always remove your jacket in your office, and don it when you're going to an important meeting.

Just as Chapter 2 abounded with ways to break the most common rules for petite dressing, there is *naturally* an exception to the Rule of

There are many ways to apply the Rule of Three for a heightened image: a traditional jacket, casual sweater, dramatic shawl or scarf, or an oversized duster.

Three. Forgo a third piece when you are wearing a distinctive dress that is best left to its own devices. (An example is Jaye's two-piece dress in Chapter 9.

DIVIDE AND MULTIPLY

Congratulations! You've learned the basics of wardrobe arithmetic. Now the fun begins! It's time to toss all of your clothes on your bed and let our imaginations run wild. We're going to blend colors and fabrics. We are going to combine attitudes (two at a time, of course!). And *you* are going to discover that when you divide your wardrobe into different tops, bottoms, and accessories, you'll multiply the possible ensembles at your command. We'll want to mix and match on the bed. You should also try on your new combinations—any you feel a little dubious about—in front of a full-length mirror.

When I help petites analyze their wardrobes, I like to use the following chart. In addition to a sample chart, you'll find blanks for your own use at the back of the book. Make several photocopies to use when you do your personal wardrobe plan. Here's how the process works:

1. Take a skirt or trousers as the foundation for each ensemble, and enter it in the left-hand column of the chart. On your bed, lay out the succeeding elements of your ensemble (following the chart from left to right): a blouse or sweater, a third layer for the Rule of Three, shoes, and accessories. Apply what you know about longitude, rule-breaking, and accessories as you develop your ensembles. Look for ways to transform the mood of an outfit by using attitude. In the first example on the sample chart, a soft challis floral skirt strikes a feminine mood with the addition of a shawl, soft suede shoes, and a cameo brooch. The same skirt lends itself to a more executive look when you add navy pumps and gold-and-pearl accessories, and top it with a crisp navy blazer.

2. If you have any questions about how the ensemble will look on you, try it on. Look in the full-length mirror and consult the checklist on page 81–82. As you'll recall from Chapter 2, a single item doesn't make or break an outfit; you're looking for the overall effect of all of the elements you've assembled.

3. When you have a combination you like, write it down on your chart, along with any comments, such as "Wear strapless bra," "Wear full slip," "Good for meeting with boss," "Wore to awards banquet," "Bob *loves* this."

4. You may find an ensemble lacks a critical element. For example, the black skirt/fuchsia camisole combination on the sample chart needs just a pair of sandals to make it dynamite. Star "need to purchase" items on your chart. Later in this chapter we'll set priorities for your shopping needs.

5. Tape the completed chart to your closet door. This step may not seem necessary right after you've devised all your new ensembles, but you'll be glad you did it when you're rushed and you're trying to remember what goes with what.

PUT IT ALL TOGETHER WITH PETITE STYLE

Skirt/Pants	Blouse/Sweater	Rule of Three: Sweater/Vest/Jacket	Shoes	Accessories: Jewelry/Scarf/Stockings	Comments:
blue/taupe skirt	cream blouse	taupe/cream shawl	taupe boots	cream belt - pearls	pin shawl in place
	blue blouse	navy blazer	easy blue shoes	antique brooch	
	white blouse	black double breasted jacket	blk pumps	red pocket square - pearls	Authority plus!
black skirt	red sweater	blk/red/white scarf	blk flats	ebony/ivory necklace	
	** fuchsia camisole	black double breasted jacket	* sandals	rhinestone earrings	Great for theater

* Plan to purchase
** Looks for
on loading

TWO PLUS TWO
EQUALS TERRIFIC

Is your closet full of tailored clothes you wear for work? Soft, lacy things you couldn't resist? Bright colors? Versatile separates? Do you have a treasure trove of scarves and other accessories? No matter what's in *your* closet, the following guidelines will stimulate your imagination and help you consider every possibility. Be alert for every way you can make two plus two equal many terrific new looks.

Colors Plus Colors

As a child, I was always asked, "What's your favorite color?" The answer was, and still is . . . none! Color excites me in terms of how one color looks in relation to another color. I'm energized by color *combinations,* not individual hues. We'll be mixing colors throughout the process of expanding your wardrobe, so follow these tips to ensure that new color combinations complement each other . . . and give you maximum longitude.

✳ As you go through your closet, you will be doing quite a few color comparisons, so make sure you do them in natural light. Electric lighting has a blue, pink, or yellow cast that distorts the colors in clothing, so do your closet inventory during the day. And since most bedrooms (and especially closets) are not very bright, take your garments to the window to make accurate comparisons. (*Never* put together a new outfit at 6 A.M. when you're getting ready to go to work. Once the sun rises, the colors may appall you.)

✳ When you mix colors, consider items in neutrals, (black, white, camel, navy, gray) that can be sparked with the other colors in your wardrobe. Add punch to understated neutrals with accent colors, such as coral with brown, red with a black-and-white herringbone, teal blue with navy, bright green with gray. You will gain longitude when you add the accent on the upper torso, because it brings the eye up.

✳ Examine prints, plaids, and tweeds for secondary colors to emphasize with other separates or accessories. Do you always wear a gray blouse to match the background color of your gray/peach/white windowpane plaid skirt? Try a top in peach for a change and uplift. Just check the outfit by the window to make sure the colors look right.

✳ As you learned in Chapter 1, you will look good in complementary colors of the same intensity. For a great look, mate a pale top with a pale skirt or trousers, such as pale pink and off-white. Balance an intense color on the upper torso with a color of equal intensity on the lower torso, such as red worn with black.

✳ Navy and white is an easy and stylish combination, but I advise petites to handle it carefully. This combination keeps coming back, most often with a military or nautical theme, such as (ugh!) middy blouses. You *will* look great, however, in a navy suit and an ivory or cream blouse.

✳ Remember to repeat an accent color throughout your silhouette for balance and to bring the eye up. With a beige dress and dark brown shoes, add a necklace and earrings in the darker rather than the lighter shade.

Suits Plus Suits

Your suits represent a major investment. Let's look for other ways to wear an expensive suit to get your money's worth.

Do you have a suit that can be crossed with another suit for a more relaxed separates look, such as, a navy suit you can cross with a suit in berry to yield two unmatched jacket/skirt combinations?

Make a suit skirt do double duty, by pairing it with a sweater for a more casual feeling—a blend of executive and casual attitudes. Soften a jacket by wearing it with a skirt in a fuller, softer fabric, perhaps a floral print . . . and enjoy wearing this stylish blend of executive and feminine on a day when you're going from work to dinner out. Or wear the jacket with jeans for an eclectic look.

Look at your two-piece dresses. Do any of the dress tops blend with the suits? Could you wear a suit jacket with any of the two-piece dresses to lend a little more authority?

The smart petite will be alert here for any combinations that reduce longitude. Avoid color combinations that chop up your image and boxy jackets and full skirts that add up to too much bulk.

Separates Plus Separates

Mixing separates can be a boon to any woman's wardrobe, offering endless possible combinations. It can also present a hazard, if the result is an unfinished appearance or the skirt-and-blouse look of a schoolgirl. But with a little planning, you can turn separates into a polished ensemble.

You may be fortunate to find several items in your wardrobe in the same color family. They'll lend themselves readily to new combinations. For example, combine a pair of wool trousers, a silk blouse, and a delicately textured sweater, all in off-white. The result? A very classy combination of casual and executive, especially when teamed with pearls, sheer hose in ivory, and matching shoes. When you match colors in the same family, be aware that each color will have a blue, red, or yellow undertone. For best results, pair colors with similar undertones.

Make the most of separates in contrasting colors (red/black; red/white/blue; blue/brown) by incorporating something in which the colors are united. Your navy skirt and burgundy sweater will look sensational when you drape a navy, burgundy, teal, and rose paisley shawl over your shoulders. The shawl also provides longitude by creating a continuous top-to-bottom color line.

Scarves lend the finishing touch that pulls many outfits together. For this reason, scarves of all shapes and sizes are wonderful wardrobe extenders (see Chapter 3, "The Petite's Best Friend—Accessories"). You can combine virtually any colors in your wardrobe *as long as* they are reflected in a scarf. The same goes for jewelry. Try "uniting" a black skirt and red top with enameled earrings or a necklace in black/red/gold. They pull these separates into a real ensemble.

Fabrics Plus Fabrics

Among the clothes on your bed, look for fabrics and textures that may be coupled for a new look. Mixing fabrics is often an excellent way to incorporate two attitudes. This is an important time to use the mirror. Stiff or heavy fabrics that look fine on the bed may overwhelm your petite figure. For example, a textured blue sweater may look great with your black velvet skirt . . . until you put them on.

* If you always wear a cotton shirt under a tweed jacket, try a silk crepe de chine blouse for a touch of class and a nice mix of casual and executive attitudes.

* Enhance a color in your feminine tapestry jacket by wearing the jacket with your executive jewel-tone silk dress.

* Give an eclectic touch to your casual blue denim jumpsuit by adding a pink scarf in a shiny fabric, a shiny pink tote bag on your shoulder, and bright pink stars dangling from your ears.

* Experiment with the angora top of a two-piece sweater dress and slim, slick evening pants.

Old Plus New

Just as brides wear "something old and something new," combining old and new in your wardrobe can give fresh life to an old favorite. I'm going to ask you to put sentiment aside, however. Since we petites usually reach our full height at a young age, we often have clothes from decades past. As you consider old/new combinations, regard each older garment in light of your current or desired position in life. It could be time to retire some old friends.

* The jacket of the black and white suit that has served you well for years may still look fine, but the skirt is beginning to show signs of wear. Try the jacket with your new black trousers and red blouse—and bid the skirt good-bye.

* Give your all-time favorite sweater a new lease on life by wearing it over narrow pants and your new pair of boots.

* If you're bored with an oldie-but-goodie, give it a change in attitude and you're on your way. A classic chemise dress becomes the latest eclectic fashion when you wear it as a tunic over textured tights, or hike it up with a belt.

* Make a critical appraisal of older items in terms of quality of workmanship, fine fabric, classic design, tasteful colors, and smart prints. How has the garment worn? Over the years, some clothing loses its crispness due to laundering, or takes on an unnatural sheen

from too-hot ironing. Dark cottons may fade; fabric may pill where it rubs against itself. Clothes are certainly a major investment today, but don't make the mistake of keeping things too long. Any item that fails to measure up should be retired permanently or restricted to casual and at-home wear.

✳ Also consider fit. Fabrics often give at points of stress, and will sag or stretch. Look at the elbows of jackets of sweaters, the knees of pants, the seat of a slim skirt. If a garment has lost its shape, it won't help yours.

Day Plus Evening

It is better to be underdressed at night than overdressed for day. With that in mind:

✳ A fuchsia blouse with provocative sleeves slit from shoulder to wrist will look smashing under your black wool suit on a day when you will go from the office to the theater. But during the day, keep the jacket on.

✳ Glittery earrings look great, worn singly as a pin on the lapel of an otherwise conservative jacket—whereas the matching bracelet and necklace would be too much.

✳ Exercise moderation. If in doubt, don't wear it for business. For evening, throw caution to the wind.

MIRROR, MIRROR ON THE WALL

Have a full-length mirror nearby in order to find out how new combinations look as others see them. (How nice to know they won't be scrutinizing your wardrobe as you are doing now.) People generally see you at an arm's length or more, and colors, especially, can look quite different at that distance. Use the mirror to test any ensembles you feel dubious about, especially when you are mixing fabrics. As you view your "new" outfit, note the *overall* effect. Ask yourself:

✳ *Do I have "everything" on?* Have you remembered the Rule of Three and your third layer? If you want a very authoritative look, make the third layer a jacket. Otherwise, choose a sweater, vest, coat, or shawl.

✳ *Do the patterns yield a harmonious blend?* Pattern-mixing is new to many petites. If in doubt, stick to patterns that have been dyed to match. Consider those within a single designer's line, such as Evan-Picone, Liz Claiborne, Villager, or Jones New York. Keep it subtle.

✳ *Do colors complement one another?* Even if they don't match, are they close enough to please when you stand back and look at yourself? The strand of red you discerned in your plaid skirt may not be prominent enough to warrant wearing the skirt with a red sweater.

✳ *Do the fabrics flatter my petite body?* Be attuned to your silhouette in the mirror. A crisp cotton blouse worn as a tunic over slim matching pants looks good and produces a balanced effect. But does the same blouse overwhelm you, paired with a similarly crisp cotton dirndl? Avoid combinations that give you too much fabric to wear on the upper and lower torso at one time and combinations where the fabric is too stiff, thick, or bulky.

✳ *What accessories will I wear with the new ensemble?* Now is the time to try them on. If what you wore with "this" top or "that" skirt doesn't look right with the new combination, experiment with something different, and perhaps something bolder.

✳ *What will I wear* under *this ensemble?* Don't laugh! A gorgeous outfit can be ruined by the wrong color underwear. For example, a flesh-colored slip under a blue bouclé dress dilutes the blue; a black slip intensifies it. You should have slips in white, nude, and black. Rely on your mirror and good lighting to tell you which is most becoming. And of course, if your undergarment will be visible, make it one to be proud of, like a lacy camisole.

✳ *Finally, is the overall mood of this outfit harmonious?* If you've mixed attitudes, have you stuck to two of the four basic attitudes? You'll look great in a "softened" suit (executive and feminine), a "dressed-up" pair of jeans (executive and casual), or a devilishly feminine pair of satin pants and camisole with kooky eclectic earrings and hat. If an outfit reflects more than two attitudes, eliminate one (then use that element to create a whole new combination).

SET YOUR SHOPPING PRIORITIES

As you devise new outfits, take note of gaps in your wardrobe. Perhaps you entered them on your chart as things you'd like to purchase to complete a particular ensemble, or filed them in the back of your mind. To get the most out of future shopping excursions, now is the time to order your shopping needs.

Give priority to:

✳ Items that would go with several things in your closet

✳ Items that would make an expensive garment more wearable

In addition, consider these tips, which will help you decide which purchases to make first:

✳ Is there a primary attitude in your wardrobe? Is everything very executive? Perhaps you'd like to look for items that will give you more opportunity to express your multifaceted personality. To give your suits more pizzazz, plan to shop for some accessories that are feminine or eclectic. On the other hand, your wardrobe may be predominantly casual. Why not look for a suit, or just an executive jacket to give a more formal, authoritative look to some of your skirts and trousers? Or an ultrafeminine dress for romantic evenings away from the kids?

✳ Take another look at the Rule of Three. Do you have quite a few skirt-and-blouse combinations that a third item would elongate and invest with greater polish? Just one or two purchases—perhaps a jacket in a good neutral color and, for a more romantic mood, a shawl—may upgrade half a dozen of your current combinations.

✳ Look at your chart. Are your possibilities restricted because of a shortage of blouses? Because you have only one top to go with a particular suit? Because you own mostly prints, with few solids to mix in? By addressing the most significant gaps, you'll increase the potential of your entire wardrobe.

✳ A few colors occur repeatedly in most closets—the colors that habitually beckon us as they hang in the store. Which are yours? Brilliant reds and blues? Muted, heathery browns and greens? Peaches and corals? Do you have a preponderance of black? (Many women choose this color first because it's "easy" to mix with other colors, but beware of mixing black and black—there are hundreds of different shades.) You'll gain wardrobe mileage when you stick to your favorite colors and watch for them as you plan future purchases and build on what you already own. Note the new colors each season. You may find some new version of colors you love . . . and you'll be in style.

✳ On the other hand, do you have many colors, few of which go together? By buying some skirts, sweaters, jackets, and/or trousers in neutral shades (black, white, brown, navy, gray), you'll get more use out of everything else. Planning a basic wardrobe around a couple of classic color combinations is a good idea for any woman interested in versatility and economy.

✳ Do you own one of those rule-breaking items we discussed in Chapter 2—a big shirt, a bulky jacket—but lack the ingredients to balance it for your petite frame? Purchasing the necessary extras will make those clothes more wearable, and far more flattering to you.

✳ Take inventory of accessories to wear with these new looks. The natural silk shirtwaist dress you have tired of may only need an accessory update to renew its classic appeal.

WOMEN TO LOOK UP TO

Loretta Lynn's secrets for projecting authority are "High heels and the right clothes." This talented country singer stands 5'2½". "I try to avoid big flowered prints," says Loretta of her style. "I like dainty things, whether I want to look like Cinderella, go out for a night on the town, or be a plain old country housewife." The movie *Coal Miner's Daughter* chronicled her rise to the top of country music. She says she likes to be described as "fiery and feisty."

Put aside any garments you wish to buy for. (I like to pin notes to each item to remind me of what I am looking for.) With a good, sharp pair of scissors, you might clip fabric samples from the seam allowance or facing to take to the store with you. You could also plan to wear or carry the garment on your next shopping expedition. This careful planning is well worth it. It will improve your chances of buying something of the right color and/or appropriate attitude . . . and save you time and money in the long run.

I trust wardrobe arithmetic has helped you see your wardrobe in a whole new light . . . as containing virtually infinite possibilities for looking terrific. You've discovered how to multiply your options and develop lots of new looks, without buying a thing. As you went through your closet, I suspect you noticed things about your clothes (and yourself!) you hadn't realized before—whether it's the knack you have for picking flattering fabrics, your fondness for eclectic accessories, or the way your casual clothes blend beautifully with every other attitude in your closet.

In this and the preceding chapters, you have learned to dress with petite flair by understanding how to use line, proportion, and balance to create longitude; seeing how to break the most common rules for petite dressing, and learning the techniques for evaluating *any* new fashion ("Six Secrets for Lifelong Style"); discovering how and when to wear accessories to enhance longitude, express your personality, and make an impact; expanding the possibilities of your existing wardrobe, by applying the concepts of attitude and the Rule of Three.

I hope you are already dressing with more verve . . . perhaps trying more daring looks than you had worn before. I'm sure you are reaping the benefits in compliments and confidence. As we continue on the path to a total image, we will be returning to the concepts you have encountered in these first chapters, because they are indeed the foundation for Petite Style.

Petite Fit

Where to Find It

CHAPTER 5

Mistake-Proof Shopping

Shop is a versatile four-letter word. Window shopping, armchair (catalog) shopping, all-day shopping, shopping the sales, shopping for others, and of course, shopping for a special occasion—all these can be as entertaining as they are necessary. For example, I enjoy seeing the profusion of fabrics and colors, catching up on the changing fashions, and marveling at what goes with what. I love finding just the right blouse, one that will create three new ensembles . . . or discovering a vintage brooch at a thrift store and feeling a sense of connection to the woman who wore it sixty years ago.

I want to make shopping as much fun for you as it is for me. Whether you spend three hundred dollars on a suit or pick up a blouse on sale for six dollars, you should be happy with them. (What kind of bargain is a six-dollar blouse if you *never* wear it?)

In this chapter, you're going to become a *savvy petite shopper* by finding out *when* to shop, *where* to shop, *what* to look for, *how* to judge good fit, and *how* to make that final decision to buy. You'll learn to take advantage of the growing availability of petite fashions and the profusion of mail order shopping possibilities. And to ensure your future shopping satisfaction, I'll share what retailers have told me about what to do when you can't find what you want.

Before entering the heady world of department stores and boutiques, however, let's return briefly to your closet. Mistake-proof shopping begins with developing your ability to be a mistake-detector.

BECOMING A
MISTAKE-DETECTOR

As you went through your closet, you probably came across a few items that have been just hanging there since you purchased them. You know the ones—the clothes pushed way in the back of your closet, the things you've worn only once or twice, the last clothes you ever reach for . . . your "mistakes."

"Why did I buy *that?*" Think back to the actual shopping excursion. By figuring out how you bought your mistakes, you'll develop an unerring ability to avoid repeating them in the future.

* Did you buy an item to match something you already owned and end up with a mismatch? Next time, be prepared. If you want a blouse to wear with a particular skirt, take the skirt with you to the store. Another suggestion: To save yourself time and frustration in the future, buy a garment *and* anything you need to go with it, including accessories, in one shopping trip.

* Is a garment hanging in your closet because you just don't feel comfortable in it? Try to pinpoint the reason. Is the hem half an inch too long? Does it make you self-conscious because the strap keeps slipping off your shoulder? Maybe you hoped to lose weight and bought too small a size. Do any needed alterations or repairs, or take the garment to a tailor. It's well worth the expense if you will then get some use and pleasure from the garment. (In the next chapter, I'll describe alterations even an inexperienced seamstress can handle.)

* Did you buy something to take advantage of a sale? Perhaps the price tempted you to buy leg-o'-mutton sleeves, corduroy harem pants, or an abstract print that would look better hanging on the wall. Now you realize it's all wrong on your petite figure. If that's the case, offer the garment to your tallest friend or favorite charity and vow to exercise more restraint the next time you see that seductive "Sale" sign.

* Did you buy a garment to wear right away? Perhaps you waited until the day of the party, hoping to find something you loved, and then you had to settle for anything that fit . . . or almost fit. Petites, especially, have to shop in advance for special occasions, not only for the best selection but also to allow time for possible alterations. Promise yourself that you'll do it right the next time. As the event gets closer, you'll be able to relax, knowing you're all set to wear something that fits, flatters, and feels wonderful.

* Think now about your favorite outfits, the ones you love to wear and reach for often. What do you like so much about them? An alluring style? A swingy skirt? The energizing color? The feel of the fabric against your skin? Try to keep these same qualities in mind as you shop in the future.

WHEN TO SHOP

Some women say the best time to shop is any time! For petites, however, the best time to shop is early in the season, especially if you wear a size at either end of the size range. Stores place orders for fewer pieces in the smallest and largest sizes, so shop when you can get the greatest size selection.

Remember that when it's snowing outside, retailers are thinking spring. Seasonal merchandise tends to appear quite early in the stores—spring merchandise by March, fall merchandise by August.

WHERE TO SHOP

Where should you shop to find clothes that fit well and flatter your petite frame? The answer is . . . everywhere. Shop in department stores and boutiques. Do your shopping at home, from mail order catalogs. Try misses, petite, and even junior fashions—don't limit your options! Some petites can go back and forth between misses and petite departments. To make sure you're taking advantage of all your shopping opportunities, don't overlook misses fashions, . . . and do cash in on the petite fashion explosion.

Don't Miss "Misses"

If you are a "fringe petite"—in the 5'2"–5'4" range—you'll probably find plenty of flattering misses fashions—that is, the women's clothing shown in a variety of departments (Sportswear, Career) throughout a typical department store. Some misses manufacturers' garments will fit you better than others. More power (and more choices) to you. For those of us who are shorter, misses is an excellent source for items such as two-piece dresses, knits, and dresses without a defined waistline, all of which adapt well to petite proportions.

To get the most out of shopping in misses, pay special attention to fit. Because of differences in design and style, some misses garments will fit you much better than others. (Later in this chapter, I'll tell you what to look for to guarantee good fit.) And promise yourself that you'll do the simple alterations that make a subtle but important difference in how a garment looks on you. Raising a hem an inch or moving a cuff button to keep a longish sleeve from falling onto your hand can make you look and feel confident and polished. In the next chapter, I'll discuss many easy alterations that will turn "good" fit into "perfect" fit.

The Petite Fashion Explosion

As far as I'm concerned, the *really* exciting news for petites is the veritable explosion in petite fashions. Over four hundred manufacturers now make petite clothing, compared to forty in 1979. Most major department stores have created petite departments. Petite-proportioned fashions can also be found in boutiques and in mail order catalogs.

(For a complete list of mail order sources, see the "Petite Shopper's Directory" in the Appendix.)

What can you expect to find in petite departments, boutiques, and catalogs?

✳ Sizes that range from 2 to 14, and occasionally from 0 to 16. This is an important point, because there is a misconception that "petite" refers exclusively to the smallest sizes. Actually, petite fashions reflect the difference *in height only* between shorter and taller women. Virtually any woman 5'4" and under should be able to find petite clothes that fit well.

✳ Prices that range from couture to moderate.

✳ Selection that runs from career to sportswear to evening, with emphasis on career and sportswear.

✳ Increasingly, fashions from major designers who have introduced petite lines. Some of them are profiled in the Appendix.

Those are the basic features of any petite store or catalog. I'd also like to share with you some highlights of the conversations I've had with retailers around the country.

Many stores give you more than just merchandise. Some offer special programs or services for the petite woman, including personal shoppers, fashion shows, and seminars. Some even put out catalogs aimed directly at petites to help streamline selection. You may be able to have your name put on a mailing list for these services and events.

Many of the boutiques are owned by petite women, whose comments enlightened and inspired me. Elizabeth Volin (5') decided to open Petite Pleasures in New York City after she spent $180 on a suit, added $50 in alterations, and found it still didn't look right. Nancy Soulé (5') of C'est Soulé in Encinitas, California, quipped. "I got tired of looking for things that fit . . . and finding things that didn't." Nancy Barisof (4'9"), of Barisof in Seattle, Washington, likes to help petites try more daring looks. She told me, "One of my strongest intentions is to break down barriers. I'll tell a woman, 'Look, I'm 4'9". If I can wear it, you can wear it, so go try it on.' "

Everything in Texas is reputed to be huge, but the Abbreviations boutiques in Houston, Dallas, and Austin have wooed petites by rethinking store design. All racks, hooks, and even counters are scaled to the petite woman. "There's nothing more intimidating than not being able to take a dress down from a rack that's too high, or having to reach up to a counter to write a check," said owner Scott Shively. Let's hope this innovation becomes the norm.

WHAT TO LOOK FOR

If you're like me, when you shop, you want it all! Unfortunately, most of us don't have unlimited resources, so we need to focus on items that give us versatility and longitude. For the best investments for petites, consider the following:

Ensembles

If you invest in a major wardrobe addition such as a suit, make the most of your shopping expedition and complete the outfit. Purchase hose in a tone similar to the skirt, and select accessories while you have the garment in hand. Give yourself some options to dress the suit up or down. For instance, you might buy a pullover sweater to layer under the new suit jacket or to wear with the skirt alone for a more relaxed look. Buy all pieces at the same time in order to coordinate colors and styles.

Many designers do the job of creating ensembles for us, with dyed-to-match colors, complementary fabrics, and coordinated prints. They may offer a skirt, jacket, and pants to mix or match, as well as blouses and sweater vests, all built around a key color scheme. This makes it much easier for the petite to achieve longitude with a line of similar color tones from shoulder to hemline.

Third Layer

Keep in mind the Rule of Three from Chapter 4 as you shop. Look for jackets, sweaters, coats, and capes to wear as a third layer for polish and presence. For the best buys, go for colors and styles that can be worn with several things in your closet.

Up!

Garments that guide the eye upward are always good investments for the petite woman. Look for detailing around the shoulder area: buttons, epaulets, pockets, collar, or color interest. Make accessories such as scarves, hats, earrings, pins, and necklaces staples in your wardrobe.

Hose

Take advantage of hosiery sales to stock up on a variety of shades, so you can wear light hose with light-colored skirts and pants, dark with dark. It's a wise investment, with inches to gain in a long look.

JUDGING FIT IN THE STORE

In the fitting room, note which designers' fashions fit you best. Each designer has a different image of its customer. The Liz Claiborne woman has a different body—literally with different proportions—than the Evan-Picone woman. Sizes may also vary dramatically, because ready-to-wear clothes do not use standardized sizing. One company's size 8 may be another's size 4. So you need to be flexible in selecting your size.

To cite Mae West once again, you generally want your clothes tight enough to show you're a woman, and loose enough to show you're a lady—and to fit comfortably. If you enjoy oversized fashions, they should still fit in terms of basic design features, such as the shoulder and the sleeve length.

PETITE FIT

You know it's too big when . . .

Shoulder pads keep slipping down your back.

Bottom of dress zipper hits your tailbone.

Neckline or front closing gapes open.

Darts and/or the waistline fall lower than they should.

Straps fall off your shoulder.

Sleeves fall over the palm of your hand.

Sweater hangs loosely, rather than gently hugging hips.

Neckline is cut too generously and bra straps show.

There is too much gathered fabric under belt.

Pant curve is too full at hip, so you feel like you're wearing jodhpurs.

Ripples appear where garment should lie smooth—through torso or across chest and back.

You know it's too small when . . .

Blouse or dress gapes in front between the buttons.

Stress occurs across buttocks or at the side pocket of pants or skirt.

Shirt or dress pulls across the back.

Fit is snug under arms or in crotch seam.

Skirt rides up as you sit.

Garment is form-fitting rather than figure-flattering.

JUDGING FIT BY MAIL ORDER

Many petite women avoid purchasing clothes by mail because they can't see, feel, or try on the garments. It *is* difficult to judge the fit of clothes seen in a drawing or a photograph, as the garment may be pinned on the model beyond the range of the camera eye. The problem is compounded if the model herself is not 5'4″ or under. Without something in the photo to lend perspective to her height, like a chair, you have little clue as to how the garment will look on your petite frame.

However, there are some clues to watch for in the picture and the written description.

Pay Attention to Construction Details That Affect Fit

✳ If the shoulders are extended, they will probably extend on you, too.

✳ Is the sleeve set-in or raglan? Perhaps you prefer the roomier fit of a raglan.

✳ Is the dress a chemise, or does it have a fixed waistline? If you are long-waisted, you may prefer the former.

✳ Do the pants have an elastic waistband, or are they trouser-style with pleats and fly-front? You may know from experience that one or the other style is more becoming to you.

Read the Description Carefully

✳ If the fabric is 100 percent cotton, you can count on the garment shrinking, and you may need a larger size than if the fabric is preshrunk.

✳ Does the description say "One size fits all?" Beware! That usually means, "One size fits all-but-petite!"

✳ Notice the manufacturer. If it's one you're already familiar with, you may know how their clothes tend to fit you.

✳ Is the catalog aimed at the general population or geared expressly toward petites? The latter is apt to have more experience in fitting petites and will offer assistance in ordering the correct size. Some catalog companies print size measurements for their private label clothes.

If you should get a garment that fits poorly in spite of your best precautions, rest assured that you can return it (except swimwear or lingerie) for a refund or credit, as provided by federal law.

For information about ordering catalogs from stores and mail order services, consult the "Petite Shopper's Directory" in the Appendix.

HOW TO BUY

Shoppers usually make purchases on the basis of four factors—fit, color, style, and price. Often price is the pivotal element while we are in the store. But when we're looking in the closet, wondering what to wear, we make the decision based on fit, color, and style. The moral: Spend a little more on something you really like. You'll get your money's worth with frequent wear.

Ask yourself these questions when you consider a purchase:

✳ *Does this garment flatter my petite figure?* In your mind, run through the longitude checklist at the end of Chapter 1. Take a mental inventory of the print and styling proportions, the elements of vertical line and continuous color, and the drape of the fabric.

✳ *Does it fit my lifestyle?* That is, will you have sufficient occasion to wear this item?

✻ *Is this garment sophisticated enough for me? Does it fit the image I'm trying to achieve now?*

✻ *Is the quality of the workmanship evident?* Look for buttons anchored securely, lining without puckers, smooth seams, and a straight hem.

✻ *Will this item require additional investment?* If so, make a decision to commit that extra money . . . before you buy. Consider accessories, costly cleaning maintenance, and alterations (see box that follows).

✻ *Will it go with something I already have?* It's nice to get a head start on a new ensemble by buying something for which you already have shoes or a blouse. I like to buy in terms of my total wardrobe, rather than piecemeal.

✻ *Does it feel good?* You'll wear it more and feel better yourself if the fabric doesn't scratch, the neckline doesn't bind, the stirrup doesn't cut underfoot. Consider how the garment will feel after you've worn it for eight hours . . . not just how it feels during ten minutes in the fitting room. For instance, synthetic fabrics that don't breathe can make you feel stifled after a few hours, whereas you can probably wear sensuous silk all day and all night.

SPEAK UP FOR FASHION

As I've said before, Petite Style has to do with how you look . . . and with the impact you make on the world. Petites have already made a significant impact on the fashion industry: The explosion in petite fashions is the result of petite women—you and me—telling stores and designers what we wanted. As the ad says, we've come a long way. *And* it's a continuing process.

If you are ever about to leave a store empty-handed, ask for the manager. Tell her what you would like to see in the store, whether it's more sophisticated petite clothes, a better selection of accessories, more funky clothes . . . whatever *you* desire. Retailers stress that they want to hear from us and will take action based on our requests. "Speak with people in the store—sales associates, the department manager, the store manager. That's how we get our best feedback," says Jessica Mitchell of Saks Fifth Avenue. Robbi Kraft, of Bullock's, recommends writing "a letter that will count. Make it well-written, type it, and address it to the store general manager. . . . Enough of these will make an impact."

Now *that's* Petite Style.

You now have 95 percent of what you need to know about shopping. The other 5 percent? It's using shopping trips to practice your techniques for lifelong style. Of the "Six Secrets for Lifelong Style" in Chapter 2, four apply to shopping. By putting them into practice when you shop, you will not only make wise investments in

Sometimes the cost of alterations is well worth it. Listen to Ellen (5'3"): "If I pay two hundred dollars for a jacket, I'll invest ten or twelve dollars to have it fit perfectly, and therefore I feel it's a thousand-dollar jacket." When you're wondering whether to purchase a garment that will need alterations, consider the cost of the garment, how much you expect to wear it, and the nature of the alterations required.

If it doesn't fit, should you buy it anyway?
Yes, if the needed adjustments involve:

IF IT DOESN'T FIT, SHOULD YOU BUY IT ANYWAY?

✳ Elastic waistband

✳ Rehemming (without distorting the line of garment)

✳ Sleeve length

✳ Taking in side seams

✳ Shortening straps

Be wary of buying a garment that doesn't fit if:

✳ The fabric is very sheer, or leather, or a sweater knit.

✳ The seams are top-stitched or flat-felled (as in jeans).

✳ There is no room to let out seams.

✳ The crotch is too low.

✳ Details occur at the point of a needed alteration; button tabs, pockets, pleats, lining, cuffs, and darts compound alterations.

In all these instances, you will have higher tailoring costs—and may want to pass up the garment.

In the next chapter, you'll find many tips about altering the most common areas in which petites have problems with fit. If you're not sure what alterations will be needed, consult with the store seamstress or a tailor.

your wardrobe—you'll also reap the benefits in long-term style. The next time you shop, remember to:

✳ *Train your eye.* In a store, you're surrounded by styles, fabrics, colors, and new ways of combining things. When you see a new look that appeals to you, visualize it on you. Try out half a dozen new fashions in your mind's eye.

※ *Experiment with rule-breaking looks.* It doesn't cost anything until you buy it, so take an armload of clothes into the fitting room and try them on.

※ *Learn from other petites.* As you see other petite women in the store trying things on in the dressing rooms, notice what they're wearing and how it looks on them. If you see a new, rule-breaking look you'd like to try, you're in the perfect place to give it a test.

※ *Keep current.* There's nowhere better than a bustling shopping mall to take mental notes on the newest fashion trends. What's being shown on the mannequins? What are the saleswomen wearing? Treat yourself to an afternoon or evening show of the season's new fashions. You'll have fun, and you'll stay on top of the new styles.

With that, give yourself 100 percent for shopping with Petite Style.

CHAPTER
6

Made to Order

In the last chapter you learned how to shop for clothes that fit you well. But you deserve even more than that—clothes that fit you *perfectly*, garments tailored to your individual figure and your personal likes and dislikes about how you wear your clothes. Perfect fit can be yours, and with a minimum of effort and cost. I'm going to show you how to achieve it.

With the increase in the availability of petite fashions, it's no longer necessary to perform major surgery on clothes you buy. Nevertheless, there are still times when the woman with Petite Style has to pull out needle and thread—or visit her favorite tailor—to fine tune a garment. After all, every petite body is different. Two women who both wear size 6 may differ markedly in individual proportions. They may also differ in the way they like to wear their clothes: One woman likes skirts that hug her hips, another abhors anything that binds.

In this chapter, I'll guide you step by step through more than a dozen simple alterations and help you decide which alterations are best left to a tailor. Even if you are an inexperienced seamstress, you should be able to do many alterations, however. I'll tell you how you can add designer touches to your wardrobe for a fraction of designer costs. And if you enjoy sewing and wearing custom clothes, you'll find tips for ensuring that your finished results look as good as you had hoped.

PERFECT FIT . . . AND HOW TO GET IT

"There's nothing more embarrassing than having the Scotch tape unstick from the hem of your skirt, or screaming because the pin holding up your pants has come undone."

JILL (4'11")

We've all been there! Every woman has occasionally resorted to rolling up a skirt at the waist, rehemming with tape or safety pins, or tucking under too-long sleeves in order to wear a new purchase immediately. For the long run, however, the discriminating petite will make smoother and longer-lasting alterations. Following are tips for altering the trouble spots many petites find in clothes.

Shoulders

Good fit is critical, and nowhere so evidently as in the shoulders, since the fit at the shoulders determines how your blouse, dress, or jacket will hang on your body.

Shoulder pads, so popular in the 1940s, have come back in recent years. Some women like the reappearance of shoulder pads, some don't. Some buy pads by the dozen and even wear them under tee shirts! "I wouldn't be caught dead without shoulder pads!" exclaims Joann (5'2"). Whether you love 'em or hate 'em, some of the easiest alterations involve shoulder pads.

ADDING SHOULDER PADS

If the shoulder seam of a garment extends beyond your shoulder just slightly, you can eliminate droopiness by adding shoulder pads. You'll also create a couture appearance by sharpening the shoulder and elongating the line of the garment. You can find shoulder pads in fabric stores or department stores, sold with notions or lingerie. In the latter department, you may also find tee shirts with pads sewn in. Shoulder pads can be tacked in place with a couple of loose stitches along the shoulder seam or anchored over lingerie straps with velcro strips, which you can sew in by hand.

Select from pads intended for set-in sleeves or pads that cup the shoulder, made especially for raglan sleeves and garments with extended shoulders. They come in a variety of thicknesses (¼" to 1"). Your choice should depend on the garment and your proportions.

Shoulder pads for set-in sleeves . . .   *for raglan sleeves.*

REPLACING SHOULDER PADS

If the shoulder pads of a garment are too exaggerated for your petite proportions, remove them. Then be sure to replace them with thinner pads. Otherwise, the excess fabric provided to accommodate them will deflate and detract from a well-tailored appearance. If you can't adjust the fit in the shoulders with shoulder padding, take the garment to a tailor, as the sleeve will probably have to be removed, reset, and eased in accordingly.

SHORTENING SHOULDER STRAPS

On a camisole, gown, or sundress, this is a common—and easy—alteration. Pick open the seam, securing the straps in place (I suggest shortening straps from the back, just in case the result looks slightly less than perfect). Pull the straps to shorten them the same amount on *each* side. Try on the dress for a final check, then sew the straps along the original seam. Trim off any excess at the ends of each strap. (My husband loves to buy me lingerie, which frequently has "spaghetti" straps. Take it from me, this alteration is no big deal!)

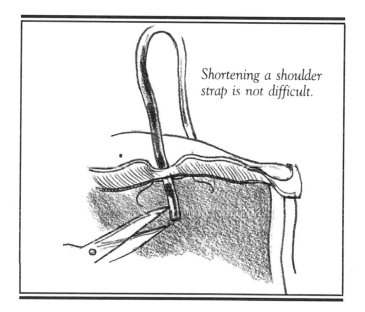

Shortening a shoulder strap is not difficult.

Sleeves

Jacket sleeves should extend to the wrist bone, blouse sleeves just slightly beyond. Often, however, sleeves on the petite extend to the thumbnail. Don't be at the mercy of a jacket in which you're always having to tuck up the sleeves. Quality fit will win hands down, so alter sleeves properly.

SHORTENING JACKET SLEEVES

Especially if they are lined or constructed of two parts with pleats or button detail at the wrist, jacket sleeves are intricate and should be shortened by a tailor.

ALTERING BLOUSE SLEEVES

If a sleeve falls down over your palm, the alteration may be as easy as moving the button on the cuff. Simply remove the button, adjust the cuff so it fits the wrist snugly, and make a mark under the buttonhole to show you where to replace the button.

If the sleeve is much too long, however, it needs to be reset by a tailor.

Reposition buttons on a cuff to prevent the sleeve from sliding down over your hand.

Waist

Waistband alterations that require more than adjusting elastic or repositioning a button (as described below) should be referred to a tailor, because they involve removing and resetting the waistband.

SHORTENING ELASTIC

To shorten elastic, open the casing seam 2″ to 3″ along the back of the garment. Pull the elastic and "pinch" it, securing it with a safety pin. Try the garment on to check the fit (sitting as well as standing). Adjust accordingly. Then cut the elastic and overlap the ends one inch. Trim as needed. Stitch through the overlap to secure, then ease throughout the casing and close the casing.

BELOW *To adjust an elastic waistband, open casing, pinch elastic, then stitch to secure and close casing.*

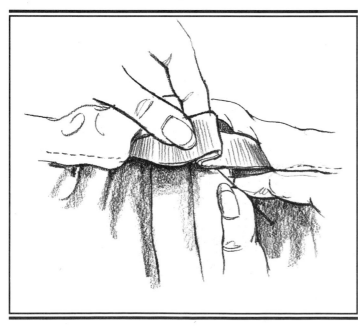

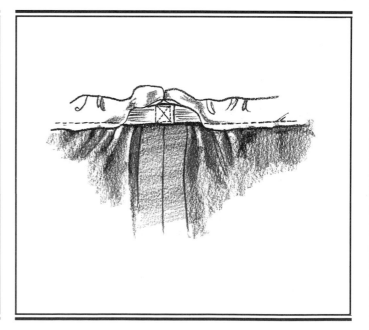

Breaking the Rules

RIGHT *You don't have to stick to one-color outfits. Just make sure you choose colors that coordinate, rather than contrast so sharply that they cut you in half.*

You can wear horizontal stripes— if they're subtle colors or serve to bring the eye up.

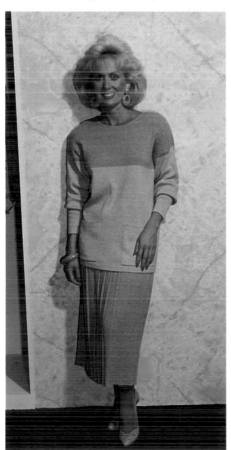

You can mix prints—provided you balance the scale and number in any one outfit.

TENÉ

CLAIRE

RUTH

▲
BEFORE

AFTER
▼

TENÉ

CLAIRE

RUTH

See pages 123–129 for details on these terrific transformations.

JAYE

TENÉ

CLAIRE

RUTH

JAYE

▲
BEFORE

AFTER
▼

JAYE

TENÉ

CLAIRE

RUTH

JAYE

CLOSE UPS *See pages 124–128 for tips on bringing out your own Petite Style.*

Four striking variations on the "rule of three"—the third layer that conveys polish and power and turns any outfit into an ensemble.

. . . *the jacket that matches the skirt*

RIGHT . . . *the jacket worn over the tailored dress*

RIGHT BELOW . . . *the jacket that dresses up slacks or trousers*

. . . *the jacket in a color that complements rather than matches a casual outfit*

MOVING BUTTONS

If you are moving the button to make the waist smaller, avoid creating a pucker, especially if the button is located above the zipper. Puckers are signals that you need more extensive alterations—and a tailor.

Torso

Excess fabric in the body of a garment can overwhelm a petite. You can absorb small amounts of fabric in the seams (an equal portion of the total in each seam, please). This is an easy task, as long as the seam is not topstitched or flat-felled (as in jeans) and doesn't include a zipper or pocket. (In case of any of these, you may prefer to call upon a tailor.) The important thing to remember is to *taper*. Try on the garment and pin the seam at the widest point. Work from that point out in each direction to the original seam, gradually tapering as you go along. Otherwise you'll get a staircase effect that ruins the style line of the garment.

Crotch

If the crotch depth in shorts or pants is uncomfortably short, you can lengthen it fairly easily. Find the curved seam that runs from center front to back. Start at the original seam in the front, just below the zipper if it's a fly-front, or 3″ to 4″ up from where the leg seam intersects the crotch seam. Gradually deepen the seam to ½″ at the seam intersection, then taper an equal distance to the original seam in back. Try on the garment, then trim away excess seam allowance.

If the crotch falls too low, there is little you can do without removing the waistband—a job for the tailor.

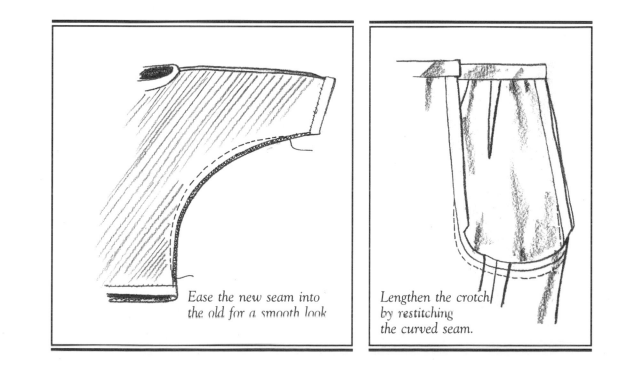

Ease the new seam into the old for a smooth look

Lengthen the crotch by restitching the curved seam.

Pockets

It's such a nuisance to have to rely on a purse to carry everything. Pockets let you pick up and go with such freedom. I love clothes with pockets . . . especially when I can reach them! Unfortunately, a petite woman occasionally discovers pockets hovering about her knees. Wearing a belt and creating a blouson (blousing on the top) effect helps at times, but it's not difficult to raise a pocket in the side seam.

RAISING SIDE SEAM POCKETS

Carefully open the seam at the front and back of the pocket and continue opening for a couple of inches above the top of the pocket. If both side seams have pockets, be sure to raise each the same distance. Pin them in place and try on the garment to check positioning, then restitch the seams.

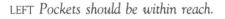

LEFT *Pockets should be within reach.*

BELOW *Pockets in the side seam can be raised easily.*

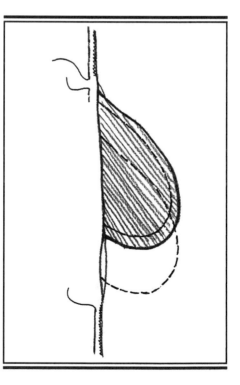

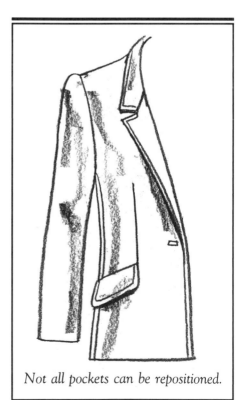

Not all pockets can be repositioned.

RAISING OTHER POCKETS

Judge before you buy! Patch pockets are not difficult to raise. However, in some fabrics the original stitching will show, so raising the pockets is not advisable. Welt pockets cannot be repositioned, as the fabric of the garment has been slashed.

Hem

If you have several alterations to make on a garment, save this for last, since other alterations may affect the overall length. (If you are taking in side seams, you often have to open the hem anyway.) You may be tempted not to bother raising a skirt or trousers "just a hair," but half an inch can make a big difference in the garment's appearance and appeal. When you're trying on the garment, wear the undergarments and shoes you expect to wear with it. See pages 32–33 to help you determine the most appropriate skirt length.

SHORTENING AT THE WAIST
In some cases, the waist is the best place to shorten a skirt, especially if the garment is a knitted skirt with an elastic waist. Open the casing at the waist and remove the elastic. Try on the skirt, holding it in place with the elastic encircling your waist on the *outside* of the skirt. Experiment until you have the length you want. Now mark a new position for the casing, keeping it the same depth as before and trimming any excess. Sew the casing seam, leaving space to insert the elastic. Then insert the elastic and close the seam.

SHORTENING AT THE HEM
First open the hem. Position your shoulders and waist comfortably, and stand erect, with your weight balanced on both feet. Have a second person mark the desired length, using a yardstick with tailor's chalk or straight pins. Pant lengths may also vary, depending on style and on fashion trends. Pants should *not* be so long that they sag in the front creases. The way pants fall is also greatly affected by the height of your shoe heel.

After you have the hem pinned up evenly all the way around, remove the garment. At this point you may have to trim away excess fabric in the new hem to allow the skirt to hang smoothly. The depth of the hem depends on the type and amount of fabric, but usually you won't want more than two inches. Use the original hem as a guide. Check that the seam(s) in the hem align with the seam(s) above and that you have no puckers along the edge of the hem. You may press the fold of the hem lightly, but do not press over pins, as they may leave a mark, and do not form a crease, in case the hem is incorrect. Try on the garment again for a final check. Finish the raw edge of the hem in any of the following ways: by turning under ¼″ (on lightweight fabrics only); with seam binding; or by machine stitching. You are now ready to sew the hem, preferably by hand, using a blind stitch— that is, catching only a few threads from the right side of the fabric, so the stitches do not show.

GO TO THE TAILOR!
If your skirt is pleated or made of a delicate fabric with a rolled hem (as on a scarf), you might take the opportunity to become acquainted with a tailor, as these items will prove more difficult. I also strongly suggest having coats and jackets hemmed professionally, because lin-

ing, front facings, hem stabilizers, and heavy fabrics complicate the procedure.

PERSONALLY YOURS

If you're like me, your taste runs to couture but your budget runs more to off-the-rack. In that case, this section is for you. You can add distinctive touches to ready-made clothing for a small amount of money and effort, and with a minimum of sewing experience. Here's how to pay a small price . . . and get a custom-look garment:

＊ Buttons are a minor investment for a great return. Consider the selection: jeweled buttons, wood buttons, ivory, mother-of-pearl, Oriental love knots, brass, silver, pewter, hand-painted, imported, monogrammed. And they come in every color imaginable. You can upgrade a blazer just by replacing the standard plastic buttons with rich imported gold. Change just the buttons, and you can change the whole attitude of a garment. New buttons can give you new color combinations; for instance, changing the matching plastic buttons on a blue dress to black mother-of-pearl. I extended the wear of a black linen coatdress that had rhinestone buttons. When I tired of wearing it for evening, I exchanged the rhinestones for natural wood buttons and gave the coatdress a new lease on life. The possibilities are endless. Just be sure when you select new buttons that they will fit through the original buttonholes.

＊ Make yourself an eye-catching scarf for a fraction of the cost of a ready-made scarf. Ask a salesperson to help you select a fabric such as wool challis that you can fringe (no sewing required!). Cut it in a large square or oblong shape, in a size proportionate for you. To create the fringe, just pull out as many threads as you want at the ends. I have several of these, which I wear as shawls, in a beautiful array of colors and patterns. To me, a soft wool print scarf is a must-have.

＊ Add a finished touch to a continuous line of color. Just browse through the notions section for belt kits and buckles for tailor-made belts, requiring no sewing. With so many fabrics to choose from, you're sure to find several that complement or blend with the color of your outfit. You can also braid or finger-crochet a belt for a special outfit— just look for strips of leather and trim. (See "Scarf-Tying Techniques" in the Appendix to learn how.)

＊ So you want to make an entrance at an evening affair? With a little easy sewing, you can. Leave it to a sequined tube top (with just one seam) to dress up a suit for evening. Add spiffy rhinestone studs to the shoulder yoke of a top or a jacket. Or make a "fan" out of flocked black netting to wear in your hair. For an eye-catcher that requires no sewing, consider a boa, available in notions departments in any length.

＊ Lace collars or beaded appliqués will add sparkle to a plain dress, blouse, or sweater. To turn a simple outfit into a holiday sensation, trim the edges of a white jacket with beaded trim; or outline a plain neckline with gold sequined appliqués. Sew them on easily by hand with a few running stitches around the edge (from underneath, please). Just be sure to position them correctly with pins first.

✳ I bought a green lamb's wool sweater because in my house we celebrate St. Patrick's Day. Come the holidays, I wanted a Christmas outfit, so I added pearlescent epaulets to the sweater and reaped all kinds of compliments. I later wore the epaulets on a winter white suit.

Beaded appliques add a designer touch.

WOMEN TO LOOK UP TO

"Maybe being short makes you feisty," says **Apollonia Kotero.** "But I'm out to break the rules. None of this small-scale stuff for me—I'm light-years away from demure prints and delicate jewelry!" Rock star Apollonia, 5′4″, starred in the film *Purple Rain* (opposite Prince) and portrays herself on TV's *Falcon Crest.* Her dazzling face and figure also appear in *McCall's* June 1986 pattern catalog—in five outfits on which she collaborated with *McCall's* designers.

CUSTOM MADE FOR THE PETITE

For the petite woman who wants the ultimate selection of style, fabric, and quality, custom-made clothes are the answer. Whether you do the sewing yourself or you're lucky enough to have a seamstress locked away in a private room, sewing offers you the opportunity to fit clothes to your body, your personality, and your lifestyle.

Selecting the Right Pattern and Fabric

To select a pattern appropriate for your petite stature, follow the same principles as for all petite-flattering clothes:

✳ Select styles that will give you a long line (following the same guidelines as in Chapter 1).

✳ Watch proportion. Avoid overwhelming details and styles or fabrics with excessive fullness.

✳ If you use a printed fabric, look for a print size proportional to the size of the garment and to you.

Selecting the Right Size

Just as with clothes "off the rack," good fit is critical in custom-made garments. Unlike ready-made clothes, however, pattern sizes *are* based on standard measurements. Be aware that the size you wear in ready-made may differ from the best pattern size for you. To determine the right size pattern for you, compare your height, your back-waist length, and bust, waist, and hip measurements to the size chart below. If you're buying a misses pattern, choose the size that comes closest to your bust, waist, and hip measurements. Do you fall between sizes? Petites should usually choose the smaller size. Another plus of sewing is that you can make refinements in fit for your particular figure, so you can, for instance, use one size for the top of a garment and another for the bottom.

MISSES' PATTERN SIZE CHART

PATTERN SIZE	2	4	6	8	10	12	14
BUST	28½" (72cm)	29½" (75cm)	30½" (78cm)	31½" (80 cm)	32½" (83cm)	34" (87cm)	36" (92cm)
WAIST	21" (53cm)	22" (56cm)	23" (58cm)	24" (61cm)	25" (64cm)	26½" (67cm)	28" (71cm)
HIP	30½" (78cm)	31½" (80cm)	32½" (83cm)	33½" (85cm)	34½" (88cm)	36" (92cm)	38" (97cm)
BACK WAIST LENGTH	15" (38cm)	15¼" (38.5cm)	15½" (39.5cm)	15¾" (40cm)	16" (40.5cm)	16¼" (41.5cm)	16½" (42cm)

MISSES' PETITE FIGURE MEASUREMENT CHART

PATTERN SIZE	6	8	10	12	14
BUST	30½" (78cm)	31½" (80cm)	32½" (83cm)	34" (87cm)	36" (92cm)
WAIST	23½" (60cm)	24½" (62cm)	25½" (65cm)	27" (69cm)	28½" (73cm)
HIP	32½" (83cm)	33½" (85cm)	34½" (88cm)	36" (92cm)	38" (97cm)
BACK WAIST LENGTH	14½" (37cm)	14¾" (37.5cm)	15" (38cm)	15¼" (39cm)	15½" (39.5cm)

Sewing with Petite Patterns

Just as manufacturers of ready-made clothes now design for petite women, the major pattern companies offer patterns specially marked for petite figures. I enjoy sewing with these because they're so easy to follow.

❋ *Vogue* offers many regular patterns as small as sizes 2, 4, and 6 by special order. Also available are numerous petite-proportioned styles by designers such as Calvin Klein, Perry Ellis, Ralph Lauren, and Oscar de la Renta. Both small-size and petite-proportioned patterns are noted in the back of the counter catalog.

❋ *Butterick* patterns designed for the woman 5'4" and under are coded in the back of the counter catalog. Needed adjustments are printed on the pattern tissue. Designers include Richard Warren, Ellen Tracy, and J. G. Hook.

❋ *McCall's* patterns are "petiteable," with needed adjustments printed on the pattern. *McCall's* patterns include styles from petite designers Liz Claiborne, Laura Ashley, and Eklektic Dresses. Petite entertainers Apollonia Kotero and Shari Belafonte-Harper model fashions in the counter catalogs.

❋ *Simplicity* also offers mature styles from their misses line for the petite woman, with special altering instructions conveniently marked on the pattern. Oleg Cassini, Cathy Hardwick, and Gunne Sax designs are adjustable for Miss Petite.

Adjusting a Misses Pattern

If you fall in love with a fashion that doesn't come in a petite size, don't dismay. You can alter any misses pattern, as long as you're aware that there's more to it than just chopping off the hem. The petite figure generally measures the same as misses in the bust and hips, but petite proportions are more compact. That is, as you can see on the size charts, the distance between bust, waist, and hips is less. Therefore, you need to break the total pattern into segments and reduce it proportionately to fit not just your height but your figure contours as well. Use the following guidelines.

❋ Remove excess length *throughout* the pattern. Since petites have a back-waist length 1" shorter, remove ½" at the armhole level and the other ½" between the waist and bust. A petite's finished garment length is 2" shorter. Do this adjustment in two parts—between the waist and hips and between the hips and hem.

❋ Crotch depth (from waist to crotch) is ½" less for petites. Adjust pants and shorts patterns accordingly.

❋ Shorten full-length sleeves a total of 1-¼", in three *equal* parts: in the sleeve cap, above the elbow, and below the elbow.

✳ Draw all adjustment lines at right angles to the grainline arrow so the finished garment will drape properly, on the grain.

✳ When you fold and tuck the pattern pieces to make adjustments, check to be sure the grainline remains straight.

✳ Don't forget to make matching adjustments on the front and back pattern pieces and on any front facings or neckline area pieces such as collars. Respace buttonholes if necessary.

✳ Typical petites measure ½″ larger in the waist than the corresponding misses pattern size. To adjust for this, add ⅛″ in each side seam and taper the new cutting line into the original. Adjust the waistband accordingly.

✳ To be sure that the garment is perfectly proportioned for you, read the garment description on the pattern envelope to determine the amount of design ease allowed. Be prepared to alter styles with exaggerated details such as broad, extended shoulders and roomy dolman sleeves, as well as boxy, oversized fashions. You may have to remove excess width in the shoulders or through the torso, remembering to do so on both the front and back pattern pieces.

✳ As you customize a pattern to your figure, don't forget to scale down details such as pockets, tabs, collars, and lapels.

Special Tip: I'm apt to use a pattern several times, often changing the neckline, sleeves, or skirt. Therefore, I make my pattern adjustments with the removable tape that is intended for typing corrections. When I want to change the pattern later, the tape lifts off easily.

With these pattern adjustments, you can enjoy a wide range of fashion trends, and keep it all in proportion.

IN THE FABRIC STORE

To get the most out of your trips to the fabric store, follow these pointers:

✳ As you browse through pattern books, evaluate patterns for their potential to add longitude. Keep in mind vertical seams and detailing. Look for specially marked petite-proportioned patterns.

✳ When shopping for fabric, take along the fabric chart in Chapter 1. You'll avoid spending valuable time and money on a fabric that won't complement your figure.

✳ Partially unroll a bolt of fabric and hold it up to yourself, looking into a full-length mirror to judge the overall effect.

✳ Take this opportunity to blend colors and mix prints successfully. Arrange two or more bolts of fabric together, then check the mirror to see how the combination looks against your body proportions.

✳ Look at the pattern layout to calculate savings before you purchase your fabric. As a petite, you are apt to require less yardage than called for on a pattern envelope.

✳ Purchase buttons and shoulder pads that are petite-proportioned, too.

Special Tip: When you don't have much time to sew, choose a simple (fast!) style, then splurge on elegant fabric . . . for stunning results.

Now that you realize how easy it is to customize your clothes, I hope you will "design" some of your own . . . and enjoy wearing an "original."

Earlier on your journey to Petite Style, you developed Petite Flair. You mastered the concept of longitude, learned how to break the rules, and made friends with accessories. You discovered how to create an exciting new wardrobe without having to buy a thing.

Now you know how to continue the process when you add new things to your wardrobe. Here and in Chapter 5, you've seen how to achieve perfect Petite Fit, whether in the store, through the mail, or sitting at your sewing machine.

As you put Petite Flair and Petite Fit into practice, you will create couture looks that proclaim, loud and clear, your Petite Style.

Petite Polish

Adding the Finishing Touches

CHAPTER
7

Options for Every Body

Years ago, a height of 5″2″ and a rounded figure were considered feminine perfection. More recently we've idealized the tall, thin fashion model; now that image is on the way out as well. I'm thrilled to see that petite women are breaking the "height barrier" for modeling. As for ultra-thinness, hurrah for the current trend toward noticeable muscles and a look of good health.

Whatever the current standards, the key to an attractive petite figure is a combination of Mother Nature . . . and Petite Polish. In Chapter 1, I talked about one aspect of proportion—selecting clothes scaled to your body. Proportion has another important meaning for petites, as well: It's using your fashion savvy to draw attention to your figure assets and minimize figure flaws.

Not even models have perfect proportions—they just *look* perfect; so Shirley (5′2″) and Karen (4′11″), two attractive professional models, admitted to me. Shirley claims she has no waist; she deemphasizes her waist area by avoiding tucked-in blouses. To compensate for a very small bust, she wears a padded bra. Karen matches belts to whatever color she is wearing on top make her look longer-waisted. She wears light-colored skirts with light, neutral stockings to downplay legs she describes as "birdlike." You could have fooled me! Even when Shirley and Karen pointed out their "imperfections," I had a hard time believing they were not simply blessed with ideal figures, because they so skillfully create the illusion of perfect proportions.

You can do it, too. In this chapter, you'll determine your proportions. You will learn how to draw the eye to the best aspects of your figure and camouflage figure problems. I'll also offer some tips for some very special petite women—mature petites and pregnant petites.

WOMEN TO LOOK UP TO

Debbie Reynolds (5′½″) has had a distinguished film and stage career, including unforgettable performances in *Singin' in the Rain*, *Tammy*, and *The Unsinkable Molly Brown*—although she almost didn't get the *Molly Brown* role. "The director didn't want me for the part. He thought I was too short for it," she remembers. "I asked him, 'How short is the part?' And I landed the role!"

Now in her fifties, she has created an exercise video for older women and is writing her autobiography. She has also served as representative for Leslie Fay petite fashion.

KNOW YOUR BODY

Being petite doesn't mean you're short all over. By examining your vertical proportions, you may discover you are relatively long-waisted or that you have long legs. As Nancy states, "I am 4′9″, slim-hipped, and thick through the middle. If I were 5′9″, I would still look good in the same style and not the others."

Whatever your proportions, knowing them will help you use the information in this chapter to look your very best. (It will also help you recognize when a garment may need some of the alterations described in the last chapter for a better fit.) As you measure yourself, remember that the term "evenly proportioned" isn't either *good* or *bad*. It only means that your measurements fall within an average range. In fact, when it comes to such things as long legs or broad shoulders, we tend to admire "uneven" proportions.

To take your measurements, you'll need this book, a pencil, and a tape measure. (You may want a friend to help with the tape measure.) Wear the undergarments and hose you normally wear; leotard and tights are okay, but do wear a bra and girdle if these are typical for you. Stand in front of a full-length mirror, preferably on a hard surface (you don't want to lose half an inch in the carpet pile). Take your shoes off and stand with your weight equally distributed on both feet.

First measure your height from the top of your head
   (*not* your hair!) to the floor and note the measurement.   _____inches
Measure the length from the top of your head to your
   hipbone (generally the widest part of the hip).   _____inches
Measure from your hipbone to the floor.   _____inches

If these two measurements—head to hip, hip-to-floor—are equal, you are evenly proportioned. If the head-to-hip measurement is greater, you are short-legged. If hip-to-floor is greater, you are long-legged.

I am   —short-legged   —long-legged   —evenly proportioned

Now measure from the crease at your underarm (do not raise your arm) to your hipbone.   _____inches

Determine where your natural waist appears and measure:
  From your underarm to your waist.   _____inches
  From your waist to your hipbone.   _____inches

An evenly proportioned waist falls halfway between your underarm and your hip. If your underarm-to-waist measurement is less than waist-to-hipbone, you are short-waisted. If you are longer from underarm-to-waist than from waist-to-hipbone, you are long-waisted.

I am   —short-waisted   —long-waisted   —evenly proportioned

We tend to be more familiar with our bust, waist, and hip size than with our vertical proportions. Still, just as measuring yourself vertically may have given you some surprises, I encourage you to measure your circumference. Don't just assume that you're thick-waisted or large-hipped. Use your mirror or a friend to look at side and back views and to make sure the tape measure lies flat against your body and parallel to the floor.

Bust. Bring the tape measure across the fullest part of your bust and straight across your back.   _____inches

Now bring the tape measure around your body just above your breasts.   _____inches

Subtract the chest measurement from the bust measurement.   _____inches

If your bust measurement is less than 1 inch larger than your chest measurement, you are small-busted. If it is 1–3 inches larger, your bust is average. If it is more than 3 inches you are large-busted. This is also a guide to cup size. Small-busted women generally take an A-cup bra, average tend to take a B or C, and those with large breasts take a D-cup or larger.

I have   —small bust   —average   —large

Hips and Waist. Enter your bust measurement from above.   _____inches

Measure your waist (no fair holding your breath!).   _____inches

Measure around the fullest part of the hips, usually seven inches below the waist.   _____inches

On a woman with "average" measurements, the hips measure two inches more than the bust and nine to ten inches more than the waist. Remember, however, that these measurements are relative. For example, if you determined above that you have a small bust, your hips may measure three inches more than your bust and still be average. Or you may have less than nine inches difference between your waist and hips, and you have an appealing, boyishly slim figure. Do use your judgment in selecting the labels below; the point is to identify special areas that you will learn to highlight or camouflage later in this chapter.

I have   —small hips   —average   —large
I have   —small waist   —average   —thick

One more aspect of proportion is the circumference of your shoulders, relative to your hips. Consider equal width average and slightly wider broad-shouldered. If your shoulder measurement is less than your hip measurement, consider your shoulders to be narrow.

Hip measurement (from above):   _____inches
Shoulder measurement   _____inches

I am   —broad-shouldered   —narrow-shouldered   —average

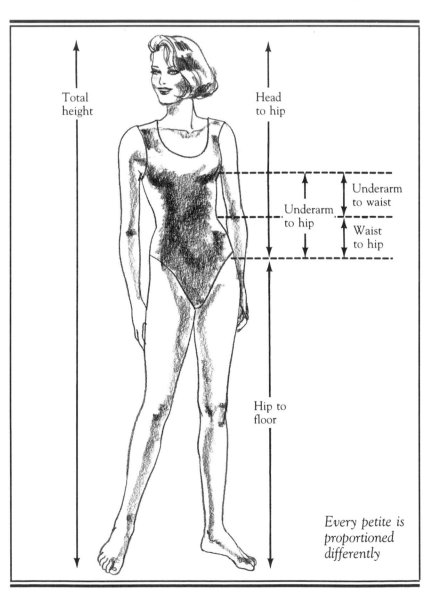

Every petite is proportioned differently

**WOMEN
TO LOOK
UP TO**

"When I read about a woman who has it totally together, my reaction is to go home and eat a carton of Cool Whip," says **Cathy Guisewite**. No one would know it, to see the 5'2", 105–pound woman whose comic strip is carried in five hundred newspapers.

However, if you read the comic strip "Cathy," you know that Cathy Guisewite hasn't forgotten the days when she weighed 150 pounds. She sympathizes with women who are struggling with such things as weight, boyfriends, parents, and careers, and she is able to convey all that with compassion and humor. No wonder the strip is so popular that there are now eleven "Cathy" books and an Emmy award–winning animated television special with the comic strip heroine.

"Cathy's" creator says she still has the same insecurities she had before she was a nationwide success, and she still has the same urge to overeat when problems arise. She jokingly says that the only difference is that now the clothes in her closet that won't fit are a smaller size.

Even though she may not feel she has it totally together, to her fans Cathy Guisewite is an accomplished petite woman to look up to.

NO BODY CAN
GO WRONG

Now put aside the tape measure. Stand back and look at yourself with an objective eye. Your overall appearance means a lot more than any measurements, so let's put your proportions in perspective. For example, you may be dismayed because you have wide hips, but are your legs on the long side? Long legs are the envy of many a petite. Or a large bust may be perfectly balanced by broad shoulders.

Just as no single element of clothing makes or breaks an ensemble, no single element of your figure will dominate your total image. When we discussed rule-breaking in Chapter 2, I introduced the idea of *compensating* for reducing longitude in one part of your outfit by emphasizing it throughout the rest of your ensemble. In the same way, you can compensate for figure flaws—and show off figure assets—by applying Petite Style.

A simple exercise will give you a feeling for how this works. Standing in front of the mirror, try on a slim skirt and a matching overblouse. Experiment and watch how your silhouette is transformed as you camouflage the waist, suggest it, define it, and accent it.

✳ Button the blouse. Belt and blouse it gently. Notice how it camouflages your waist.

✳ Pull on a skinny tee shirt or camisole and wear the overblouse open like a jacket, to suggest your waist and produce a slimming effect through the torso.

✳ Tuck the blouse inside your skirt, and see how it defines your waist and affects the line of your hips.

✳ Tie the ends of the blouse together at the waist, revealing a column of contrasting color in the tee shirt and accenting your waist.

Petite Style

You can camouflage your waist . . .

suggest your waist . . .

Petite Polish

define your waist . . .

accent your waist.

Which of the four ways to wear the blouse looked best on you? Just as you created four different silhouettes in this quick experiment, you can look great, whatever your figure assets or flaws, when you use your knowledge of longitude as follows

If You Are Petite And . . .

SHORT-LEGGED
You'll look your best when you conscientiously create a long line from waist to toe. Select skirts in styles and fabrics that drape your body

softly; don't add bulk with pleats or pockets. Develop your eye to recognize your best skirt length (don't let a hem hit at the widest part of your calf), and alter hems, even as little as half an inch, if necessary. Coordinate the color of your hem, hose, and shoes so as not to break the line. Avoid full, wide pants, especially those with cuffs, and shoes with ankle straps. Discover the marvelous, elongating effect of boots that reach your skirt hem.

LONG-LEGGED
Lucky you! You can afford to bend the rules on your lower torso and wear border prints, a flounced skirt, and cuffed pants. If you like, indulge in zany shoes—you can handle the attention on your feet. But avoid overly high heels, as they may make your legs appear spindly.

LONG- OR SHORT-WAISTED
Chemise, princess, empire, two-piece, or drop-waist dresses will always give you a flattering look. (The idea is to avoid waist definition.) To bend the rules and wear contrasting colors on top *or* bottom, a short-waisted petite should wear a belt the same color as the top, whereas a long-waisted petite should match the belt to the skirt to even out the proportions. Experiment with different length tops, jackets, and skirts before a full-length mirror to determine the best proportions for you.

SMALL-BUSTED
You can handle more bulk and layers on the upper torso, even horizontal lines. Blouson styling, pleated or gathered bodices, a cowl or draped neckline will flatter a small bust. Avoid fabrics that are too clingy. If you wear a padded bra, make sure it fits well and does not err in the opposite direction, making you top-heavy.

LARGE-BUSTED
Thin layers and lightweight fabrics will show the voluptuous petite to best advantage. Make friends with shoulder pads—they'll balance a large bust beautifully. Avoid horizontal stripes on the upper torso, too tight a fit, and jewelry that ends right at your bustline. Indulge yourself with a really good brassiere: Seek out an experienced saleswoman to ensure an uplifted, sensuous silhouette.

SMALL-WAISTED, SMALL-HIPPED
Accentuate your assets! Show off a small waist with a belt or waist accent. Select a belt big enough to be significant. You can also wear hip belts, pleats, and peplums; even hip yokes, if they're in matching or coordinating fabric. Avoid contrasting hip yokes, because they tend to cut a petite in half.

LARGE-WAISTED, LARGE-HIPPED
Remember the guidelines for longitude from Chapter 1—they'll flatter a large waist and/or hips as well. Look for vertical lines. Select thin, flowing fabrics (not stiff or clingy). Experiment to find your most

flattering silhouette—tucked in or gently bloused. Take advantage of darker colors to slim proportionately large areas. Stay away from eye-catching prints and belts, as they will give you a boxy silhouette. Balance your waist/hips with shoulder pads.

A jacket will also balance wide hips; a skirt or pants in a similar color will give you the longest line. The vertical line of lapels and a jacket edge will slim your silhouette, but avoid the added bulk of a double-breasted jacket, as it gives you two layers of fabric in front. Choose a jacket that ends above *or* below the widest point of your hips. Slash pockets are more slenderizing than horizontal or patch pockets.

BROAD-SHOULDERED

You are apt to wear clothes well because Mother Nature gave you padding where many designers add it to clothes to make them hang better. Occasionally, you may want to replace thick shoulder pads in a garment with thinner pads. You'll benefit from long scarves to emphasize vertical lines. Avoid shoulder yokes and scarves worn about the shoulders.

VERY SLIGHT

You can bend some of the rules that would overwhelm most other petites, as long as you are selective. Do strive to maintain a long line, although you can afford to add bulk to make your figure appear more substantial. Consider fabric your ally. Enjoy wearing lush, thick textures (see fabric chart in Chapter 1) and adventurous plaids. Select fisherman knit sweater, double-breasted jackets, pleated skirts, chub jackets. Go for layers of clothing (blouse-vest-jacket, for instance, or sweater-jacket-shawl). You may prefer looser silhouettes, such as a sweater dress, rather than clothes fitted to your super-slender figure.

EVENLY PROPORTIONED

There are no particular guidelines for you, nor are there any exceptions. You have many choices for bending the rules to fit your personal taste and your goals. Just remember: You can break some of the rules some of the time, but not all the rules all of the time.

As you will see in the Wardrobe Clinic that follows, you can follow the suggestions for several different areas—for example, small bust *and* long legs—to create total images that work for your individual proportions.

WARDROBE CLINIC

How alike yet different we all are. Each of the three women in the photograph is 4'11". However, you can see how much they differ from one another in their proportions, in the clothing that will give each of them the most flattering silhouette . . . and in how they should create impact. As I "diagnose" each one and "prescribe" the clothing that will look best on her, consider how you might analyze your own figure and determine the best clothes for you.

Beth

Note that Beth's head is smaller than Sara's or Joanne's, her shoulder and waist higher, her arms and legs longer. Because of these features, she would actually appear taller than the other women (such are the vagaries of proportion). With her slenderness, a delicate bone structure, and long limbs, Beth can make an impact by wearing contrasting colors on the top and bottom. However, if she wears a belt, it should match the top color. As she's a "short-waisted" petite, a belt matching her skirt would make her appear all legs. Since she's very slight, Beth can afford to wear plaids, fullness, and bulk. She need only avoid wearing overly high heels or very full skirts, since they bring attention to her very thin legs.

Sara

Sara has even proportions throughout. For the most part, she should follow the guidelines for longitude to look her best, breaking an occasional rule. Since she is average rather than slender, she needs to be cautious about breaking rules that add bulk or fullness, concentrating on creating impact with accessories instead. Sara's skirts should end either above or below the fullest point of her shapely calves.

Joanne

Joanne has hips slightly wider than her shoulders. As a "wide-hipped" petite, Joanne looks very good in a long line of color, as in jumpsuits and hose keyed to her hem. She can handle shoulder details (pads, epaulets) to balance her proportions nicely. She should avoid the bulk and fullness of pleats, waistline gathers, and hip pockets, as well as eye-catching belts and purses. I recommend that Joanne draw the eye up by adding interest—a scarf or earrings for example—at her head and shoulders.

WOMEN TO LOOK UP TO

"I found her witty, charming, perfectly informed, smart, and shorter than me," cracks the 5'2" husband of **Estelle Getty.** Ms. Getty, who says she's "somewhere under five feet," plays Sophia, Bea Arthur's eighty-year-old mother on the television hit, *Golden Girls.* A vibrant sixty-two, she needs plenty of makeup to look right for the part. (Petites always do look youthful!) She has also appeared on Broadway and won a Golden Globe Best Actress award for her performance in *Torch Song Trilogy.*

Petite Polish

BETH   SARA   JOANNE

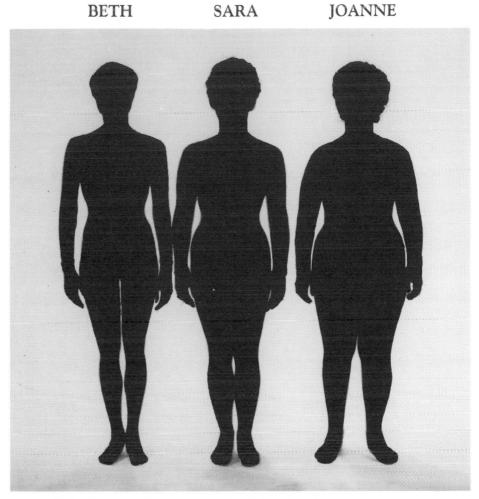

Beth, Sara, and Joanne are each 4' 11", but their proportions vary.

MATURE PETITES

Do petite women live longer? Fifty percent of American women aged 45 to 54 are petite. The percentage goes up to 64 percent for 55- to 64-year-old women, and 77 percent of 65- to 74-year-olds. One reason for the greater percentage of mature petites is that many people lose a few inches as they get older (at its worst, this tendency manifests itself in osteoporosis), so a woman who stood 5'5" at age 20 may be 5'3" at age 65. And who knows? Perhaps petites *do* enjoy greater longevity than taller folk.

Whatever the reason, as time goes on, we appreciate the fact that we petites tend to look younger longer. I'm inspired by vibrant women such as Debbie Reynolds (5'½"), who remind us that mature petites can look great and demonstrate the same energy and positive attitude as their younger sisters.

Some things do change with age, however. Many older women feel the effect of gravity. The bust and fanny droop a little, shortening the midriff and leg. The upper arm becomes rounded, and body tone starts to give a little. Other changes occur in hair color and complexion, so that colors and style that once flattered require reevaluation. If you are a mature petite, the following tips will help you look your best:

✳ Proper undergarments can help preserve a youthful appearance with an uplifted bust, trim waist, and firm hips.

✳ Evaluate the colors you have been wearing. You may wish to go to paler tones that don't overwhelm your hair color and skin. However, if bright colors look good on you, don't hesitate to wear them.

✳ Avoid exaggerated or severe styles. The suits and dark colors that give a young petite more credibility may appear harsh on you. Instead of a jacket with lapels, consider the softer look of a collarless jacket with a rounded neckline or a two-piece dress such as Jaye wears in her makeover (See color insert.)

✳ Stay current with fashion trends. Hairstyles, makeup techniques, eyeglass frames, and costume jewelry that have worked for you forever may need to be updated or retired.

✳ Do strive for longitude with vertical line and continuous color. Wear clothes that flatter you. For a thickened waist, choose outfits that do not define the waistline (chemise or drop-waist dresses, blouson tops, jackets). If you wish, wear sleeves to cover heavy upper arms. Key hose to hemline and choose low-heeled, stylish pumps.

✳ Don't cast aside new styles without trying them. A batwing sleeve may be a fun change and hide a full midriff. Shoulder pads are not *all* throwbacks to the 1940s—and they can be removed or replaced with thinner pads. Mae, a seventy-year-old petite, told me she was grateful to her daughter for the advice that just wearing her jacket sleeves pushed up could bring her in line with current fashion and give the impression of greater vitality and youthfulness.

THE SHAPE YOU'RE IN

Of course, you will look (and feel) your best if you keep in shape. Many petites have excellent strategies for staying slim, including both watching what they eat and exercising. If you are working to shed excess weight, I encourage you to use the techniques in these pages to downplay problem areas. And good luck with whatever weight control method you try.

PREGNANT PETITES

Pregnancy no longer means you have to give up the sophisticated image you've been striving to create. Petite after petite has complained to me about childish-appearing maternity clothes—ruffles, bows, and the like. Fortunately, as more professional women have been getting pregnant, designers have responded with much more stylish maternity clothes.

In the early months of pregnancy, you can take advantage of the fuller cut of nonmaternity misses fashions. But as your tummy grows larger, it will hike up the front hemline and you will need to wear maternity clothes. Unfortunately, no manufacturers at the time of this writing make maternity fashions proportioned for the short woman. Some designers do cut very fashionable clothes that are sized "Petite," but they are not specially proportioned for the woman 5'4" and under. Rather, they're equivalent to a misses size 4. So pregnant petites must be creative to look their best.

If you're pregnant, remember:

✳ Strive for good fit, especially in the shoulders. If you're having trouble with shoulder fit, choose clothes with raglan sleeves or with no shoulder seam, in which the sleeve and bodice are cut in one piece.

✳ Wear shoulder pads and oversized tops over skinny pants or leggings. Go for a fashionable inverted-triangle silhouette.

✳ Look for clothes that show off the parts of your body that don't look pregnant—that is, above and below your belly. Wear slim skirts and narrow-leg pants. Accent your neck and shoulders with keyhole necklines, jeweled buttons at your throat, contrasting collars.

✳ Make a jacket your best friend in the workplace. Remember the idea of the "mantle of authority!" Longer-proportioned jackets in particular, will camouflage your widest point.

✳ Use all of the guidelines you have learned here: Dark colors, vertical lines, and small prints will help minimize your middle. A continuous line of color will elongate as well as slim your figure, so needed at a time when you may feel as wide as you are tall.

✳ Look for two-piece dresses, particularly with the flattering blouson tops. They are adaptable on the lengthwise proportions of petites and can also be worn over pants.

✳ Splurge on accessories to wear around your face—earrings, necklaces, scarves, and hair ornaments. They will bring the eye up when you may want it there the most.

✳ Look for stylish *and* comfortable ensembles in chic fabrics. Select from attractive, contemporary fashions: metallic evening dresses or tops, rhinestone-studded sweatshirt tops, tube or trumpet skirts.

While there are only a few fashion prohibitions for the pregnant petite, they are important. Avoid:

✳ Horizontal stripes, *especially* on the upper torso

✳ Tenty styles, until you absolutely need them

✳ Stiff, bulky fabrics

✳ Anything cutesy—bows, ruffles, youthful prints. Save all that for the nursery.

✳ That popular basic of maternity wear, the jumper. While a jumper is versatile and comfortable, it projects the naiveté of a school-girl. Be the sophisticated woman you are!

Most of us are very quick to notice our figure flaws and focus on them. But now that you've had a chance to analyze your proportions, I trust that you'll give yourself credit for your assets too—everybody has them.

In this chapter, you've considered your head-to-toe appearance and learned to apply the principles of longitude selectively, to your particular body. As I promised you in the beginning of the chapter, by dressing with Petite Polish, you can create the illusion of ideal proportions . . . or is it an illusion? Only Mother Nature knows for sure! Whether you're a long-legged petite, a voluptuous petite, a mature petite, or a pregnant petite, every body looks its best . . . with Petite Style.

CHAPTER
8

Beautiful You

Beauty! Over the centuries, poets have sung about it, artists have painted it, and, if the story about Helen of Troy is true, great cities have been won and lost for it. But what is beauty? A particular shade of hair? A certain curve of the lip? Ideas of what makes a woman beautiful seem to differ from culture to culture, and even from generation to generation. Yet I believe there are certain aspects of beauty that never change . . . and that every woman can cultivate.

The universals that appear again and again have to do with *spirit*—a lively face, a genuine smile, the grace with which a woman moves. "A special smile—wonderful laughter—that's beauty," says First Lady Nancy Reagan (5'4").

A beautiful woman exudes confidence and enthusiasm. It's beauty that comes from within. It is beauty that the woman with Petite Style enhances with healthy, attractively styled hair, skillfully applied makeup, and delicious fragrance. And it becomes a magic circle. As you make the most of your natural beauty, you feel more confident and move with grace and assurance . . . which create even more of the beauty that emanates from within.

In this chapter, I want to share everything I have learned about helping *your* particular beauty radiate.

HAIR ESSENTIALS

A good hair stylist wants to make you a more beautiful woman and to ensure that you're pleased with the results. *You* want hair that is healthy, looks great, and flatters your features . . . and you want to be able to manage it with a minimum of fuss.

Finding Your Stylist

If you already have a stylist you love, congratulations! Do tell your friends about him or her; it's one of the nicest things one woman can do for another. If, on the other hand, you're shopping for a stylist, these tips will help you:

✳ Ask other women. In my mind, a good haircut is all-important, especially with the unstructured styles today. I can tell a good cut when I see one. That's why I ask women around me who does their hair. I have found two fine stylists that way.

✳ Interview a prospective stylist. Many stylists will let you come in for a free consultation, where they'll take a few minutes and discuss what you want, and how they would work with your hair.

✳ Concerned about cost? I find that spending a little more for a great cut is worth it in several ways: It looks better longer; it makes my life a lot easier in the morning; most important, a super haircut makes me feel so good.

One last, important point: Once you find a stylist you like, stay with him or her. I followed Chuck from salon to salon for five years. He finally settled down . . . three hundred miles away! Just a little too far for a cut and a blow dry. (If he'd moved only one hundred miles, I would have considered it.)

That Special Relationship: How to Get the Most from It

To create a satisfying relationship with your hair stylist, you need good communication. Whether you are just getting to know a new stylist or exploring new possibilities with your regular stylist, begin by talking for a few minutes about yourself and about what you'd like your hair to do for you.

Understand that your stylist sees women throughout the day. So make sure he or she realizes that you are a petite woman and that one of your goals is to use your hairstyle to enhance longitude. (A little later in this chapter, I'll discuss some specific petite-flattering styles.) Before your shampoo, talk about how you have been doing your hair. Other points to discuss:

✳ How adept are you at styling your own hair? Do you feel all thumbs with a curling iron?

✳ Do you prefer a "wash-and-wear" cut or weekly salon appointments?

✳ How much time do you wish to spend on your hair daily?

✳ Discuss what kind of work you do. Some styles work better for a woman in a conservative business, others for a woman in creative arts.

✳ Pay attention to other lifestyle considerations: Do you enjoy a daily swim? Travel frequently? Spend a lot of time outdoors? Do you want a style that you can glamorize for evening?

✳ Familiarize your stylist with your hair. What styles have you liked or disliked in the past? What products do you use on your hair? Is your wave natural, or chemically enhanced?

✳ The same goes for your color. Is the distinctive streak at your temple developing on its own?

Maintain an open line of communication throughout your appointment. Ask questions as you go along to enable you to duplicate the style on your own.

Together you and your stylist can determine how to flatter the shape of your face. Just as you've learned to balance your proportions through the way you dress, your hair stylist can suggest ways to balance full cheeks, a broad forehead, a sharp jawline, or a thick chin.

The right hairstyle will also accentuate your most attractive features. One way to do this: Hold your hands like a frame and, starting at your forehead, isolate portions of your face and neck to decide which features to emphasize. Do you have a widow's peak, or lovely coloration at the brow? Are you blessed with large, luminous eyes? Perhaps your ears are delicately shaped and you adore earrings. Or you have an aquiline nose, or perfectly formed lips, or a long, graceful neck. Whatever your special feature is, there's a hairstyle to enhance it.

Another thing to discuss with your stylist is hair color. Color can be a lot of fun and give you a terrific sense of freshness about your appearance. Ginny (5'2") had turned very gray. One day her regular hair stylist dashed out of the room, exclaiming, "I know what you need!" He returned with a bottle of hair coloring . . . and proceeded to color her hair auburn. Ginny loves the result; it brings out her Irish eyes.

If you've considered coloring, but felt "color-shy," be aware that there are many preparations available today that will color your hair very gently, without damaging it or giving you a "dyed" look. Some even wash out, so you can experiment with color without having to worry about maintenance. Claire's makeover in the next chapter included a lightening rinse, with super results.

On the other hand, if you've been coloring your hair for a long time, maybe you need a change. Jaye, in her makeover, went to a new, much more attractive beige shade. Lorrie (4'11") had been covering her gray for years. Recently she decided to go natural; soft gray curls radiantly suit her total image and personality.

Be aware, though, that a change in hair color may require a change in the colors of the cosmetics you use.

STYLED FOR PETITES

As a petite woman, it is especially important that you select a hairstyle that shows your sophistication. Overly simple, girlish styles can make petites look like Alice in Wonderland. To make sure your hairstyle looks as polished as you are, keep it *high,* *shaped,* and *up-to-date.*

Keep it High

Just as we dress to bring the eye up for longitude, the most flattering silhouette for a petite woman provides height or fullness at the top, the top front, or the crown. There are many ways to add fullness or volume:

* A layered cut

* Back-combing

* A permanent or body wave

* Rollers

* A curling iron

* Products such as mousses, gels, or sprays

Don't overdo it, however. You want your hair volume to be in proportion to *you.* Don't let too much height overwhelm you.

WOMEN TO LOOK UP TO

With a 5′9″ sister, **Morgan Fairchild** (5′4″) had always had a lot of incentive to stand tall. "My sister can wear whatever she wants and look great in it," says the actress. "I can't. The trick is to make people *think* I can." Among her secrets: Wearing solid colors and focusing on a single significant item (an accessory or a color.) She also scales down the volume of her blond hair in proportion to her petite size—she keeps the top short and puffy to create more lift for extra height.

Keep it Shaped

Don't let your hair become too long or too thick, because it will weigh you down. That means regular visits to the stylist; most recommend a trim every six weeks if your hair grows at an average rate. Have you always worn your hair long and can't imagine cutting it? Try a wig to preview a shorter effect. As you'll see in the makeovers of Claire and Ruth in the next chapter, new hair cuts gave both of them a tremendous boost in style.

Keep It Up-to-Date

Whether you prefer a coiffed look or an unstructured style, you owe it to yourself to update your hairstyle as fashions change . . . and as you change. How long have you worn your current style? It may look too casual for a woman striving to present a mature image. As you advance in your career, you need to upgrade your hairstyle accordingly. Or it may be time to trade in the look you've worn for many years in favor of a softer, more contemporary style.

In Chapter 9, you'll learn how much your hairstyle can contribute radiance and stature to your overall appearance.

MIRROR, MIRROR	Your most important beauty tool? It's your mirror, not only to check your side view for makeup, but to see side and rear views of your hair. Aim to look good from every angle.

PUT YOUR BEST FACE FORWARD

Beautiful faces smile out at us from magazine racks and we unconsciously think that models must look like that naturally, every minute of the day. The truth is, very few women look great without makeup.

I apply makeup every morning. Sure, I like to do it for my husband, but to be honest, it's mostly for me. I strive to be attractive, to make the most of what I have. Wearing makeup makes me feel good, ready to *face* a full day, nonstop.

Remember the Accessories Test from Chapter 3? The same way you want to wear *just the right* number of accessories, you want makeup to be *just right*—not too little, not too much. The right amount of makeup will not only enhance your features, it will also give polish to your total image. Applying that finishing touch tells others that you are savvy about your appearance—and about life in general. Wear makeup to please yourself, too. Knowing you look your best will boost your self-confidence and illuminate that inner glow.

Balance and Makeup

We've talked about the concept of balance when it comes to your clothes and your hairstyle. Your face should be "balanced," too.

* Consider your face as a whole. No one aspect should dominate. "Strong" eyes need "strong" lip color.

* Your face should also balance your total appearance. A sophisticated dress and accessories need more backup than merely powder and lipstick: Eyes need to be enhanced as well.

Daytime Makeup

I recommend a natural look for your daytime makeup, with colors that blend well with your hair and skin tones. A woman can wear a lot of makeup, if it's artfully applied. The key is not to let it *look* like a lot.

I believe there is *always* time to apply at least the bare essentials. (Women have been known to do this at stoplights on their way to work. I do *not* recommend you put on your makeup when you're actually driving.) What are the bare essentials? Powder, mascara, blush, and lipstick, for most women. The exact combination will depend on your coloring and the features you wish to enhance or downplay. For example, a redhead with blotchy skin may always want the light coverage of a makeup base to even out her skin tone. A brunette can go without darkening her eyebrows and lashes, whereas a blonde might consider mascara and eyebrow pencil absolutely necessary. A woman with deep-set eyes may not like to leave the house without a bit of concealer to cover the circles under her eyes.

If you avoid makeup for fear it will take too much time, be aware that the more often you apply it, the faster and more adept you will become. Rory (5'2") claims, "I can throw on a face in two minutes."

Evening Makeup

Go with a little heavier application and more intense color for the drama of evening dressing. This will also compensate for the artificial evening lights that tend to drain a woman's coloring.

Make your eyes dramatic. Have fun with false eyelashes and use more colored eye shadows in place of daytime neutrals. Choose shadows, blushes, lipsticks, and special creams with added iridescence for extra nighttime shimmer.

Makeup Tips

A beautifully made-up face begins with a good skin-care regimen. Cleanse thoroughly, wear moisturizer day and night, get enough sleep, watch exposure to the sun, and eat a balanced diet. Exercise, too, for that extra glow.

Do you want to catch up on the newest makeup and on application techniques? Browse through magazines or stop at the cosmetics counter of your favorite store for a demonstration. If you'd like some help developing your skill in the art of applying makeup or selecting the best colors and cosmetics for you, treat yourself to a class or a lesson at the hands of an expert at a salon. It will bring you pleasure and confidence.

The most important technique in applying makeup is *blending* your foundation, blush, and eye shadows. Use your fingertips, cosmetic sponges or brushes, or cotton-tipped swabs to blend makeup so you can't see a harsh line where any color begins or ends. Foundation and blush should be blended smoothly, especially around the hairline and neck; check your side view in the mirror. Shadow should be just that—not a distinct band of color.

If you wear glasses, you may need to compensate and wear slightly heavier eye makeup. And check your frames. How long have you worn them? Part of Jaye's makeover, in Chapter 9, involved more contemporary eyeglass frames.

You don't have to follow every makeup fad, like yellow eye-

Ah, perfume! What could be more sensual than fragrance, or more individual than your own favorite scents? I love wearing perfume, and I encourage you to indulge yourself with fragrance whenever you wish. Select a scent by trying some on your wrist, then let it mellow a bit. Don't make a decision to buy until you've seen how you like it after a few hours. Has it maintained its fragrance? When you apply perfume or toilet water, use a light hand. A *hint* of fragrance is delicious; too much, like too much makeup, spoils the effect. (P.S. I always treat myself to a spritz of a new fragrance when I walk through a department store.)

BEAUTY SECRETS

Make sure your hands speak highly of you. Well-groomed hands will guarantee a good impression with that initial handshake. Wearing polish will protect your nails. Use a clear polish or a shade that complements the colors in your wardrobe. At a time when almost every woman can have long nails, use your knowledge of proportion and don't get carried away.

Don't want to be caught off-guard? Keep an extra pair of hose (in a neutral shade) in the desk drawer at your office, along with duplicate or trial sizes of essential cosmetics and "emergency" items: breath spray, a small sewing kit, safety pins, clear polish (to stop a run), an emery board, and a pair of small scissors.

I also like to keep a small mirror unobtrusively near my desk in a closet or drawer. (I vowed to do this one day years ago, when I told the principal of my school I was on the way to a meeting and he said, "Not with that purple ditto mark on your chin, I hope!" A pre–copying machine hazard of the education industry!)

Look at your overall appearance in the mirror before you leave the house, so you'll know that your skirt is straight and smooth, your jacket shoulders are free of hair or lint, and your hose are run-free. Knowing you look your best will give you confidence and make you more beautiful.

shadow or colored mascara, but do keep current on trends—for example, more natural-looking eyebrows, lipstick pencil to reduce lipstick "bleeding," improved makeup formulas that don't fade or crease. An up-to-date appearance makes you look youthful and in style.

And remember, if you decide to try something new, with makeup it's easy to correct a mistake. Just wash it off!

You now know how to create ensembles that look wonderful on you, reflect your multifaceted personality, and give you Petite Flair. You've learned to be a savvy shopper, and to guarantee that Petite Fit is perfect fit, every time. And in the last two chapters, you have discovered how to give that finishing touch to your appearance: Dress to enhance your unique proportions and promise to give yourself the best hair care, makeup, and grooming . . . for Petite Polish!

In the next chapter, you'll see how the combination of all three adds up to a total image of Petite Style, as all of these principles are applied to four very exciting makeovers.

CHAPTER
9

From Suitable to Sensational

"Describe how you look now," I asked Andrea (5'3") when she applied for a makeover.

"Cute," she said . . . and then she added, "Yecch."

"How do you want to look?"

Andrea closed her eyes for a moment. Then her face lit up and she breathed a single, one-syllable magic word: "Chic."

When I interviewed petite women for this book, I was delighted to have several dozen accept my invitation to apply for a makeover. After all, undergoing a makeover involves risk-taking. It takes courage and a willingness to see yourself in a new light.

The women who requested Petite Style makeovers represented all ages—from twenty-one to seventy—and a variety of professions, including teachers, engineers, doctors, secretaries, newspaper editors, consultants, real estate brokers, bankers, and homemakers. We're never through growing—I also heard from several retirees. As with Andrea, I asked each woman what she wanted from a makeover. Here are a few of their replies:

"I want to show that a mother of nine children can look great."

"Now that I'm over thirty, I'd really like to become the woman in her prime, as opposed to the little girl. I want to stop being cute and become beautiful."

"To make a comfortable transition to a new maturity."

"It would be fun to see, if I were 'someone else's clay,' what they would make of me."

"I want the inside of me to show on the outside."

I was touched that so many women were opening their hearts to me, and I wished I could help each one. (All the more reason to write this book!) It was hard to limit my selection, but I did so to show women of various ages, and with a variety of lifestyles and goals.

Each of the four women I selected—Ruth, Jaye, Tené, and Claire—had a complete makeover, from hairstyle (and in some cases, hair coloring) to makeup to wearing strikingly different styles and colors than those they were accustomed to. Each woman took a risk in volunteering and putting herself in someone else's hands. It took great courage on their part to trust me. And each had great potential and charm. I helped "make the inside of them show on the outside."

As we go through the four makeovers, you'll learn how I applied the principles of Petite Style to create a total image for each woman. Before and after photographs of each woman appear in the color insert. I hope you will find aspects of their experiences that you can incorporate into your own personal style, and that you'll share my excitement at the way each woman discovered her natural beauty . . . and a new way to see herself.

TENÉ

Twenty-nine-year-old Tené (4′11″) came to me looking for more credibility. Having realized a lifetime dream to become a veterinarian, she was finding that she repeatedly had to prove herself to her human clients. She said, "People seem to think I may not be effective because I'm small" . . . especially because she prefers to work on large animals, such as horses. Tené also complained that she still had to show identification before ordering a cocktail when she went out with friends. Tené's "before" picture filled in the rest of the story: Dressed in her typical work clothes—jeans—with unruly hair and no makeup, she *did* look too young for her age and accomplishments.

I wanted to show her that she could feel comfortable and yet look as if she could handle the job (or the animal). And I wanted to capitalize on Tené's gorgeous raven hair, lively eyes, and olive complexion—and show her what a knockout she could be.

Because Tené's hair was too long and too heavy, her makeover started with cutting a good three inches off her hair. She and her hair stylist agreed that her eyes were her best feature, so they selected a style with the sides swept back to emphasize her eyes. This also gave her some lift and height on top, so important for a petite. We also relaxed the curl in her hair, making it more manageable and giving her greater control over it. As Tené demanded, this is an easy-care, unstructured style. On a daily basis, she only has to apply some gel, blow-dry the front, and let the back dry naturally.

In the hands of a makeup artist, Tené went from cute to glamorous before our eyes. After applying base—with lighter coverup to even out the color of her skin—we used burgundy blush to contour her cheeks. We blended several shades of eye shadow on her lid for a sultry effect. Although unaccustomed to wearing makeup, Tené vowed to continue with it on her own, using a modified version for every day.

Bright colors make Tené sparkle, so we put her in casual but professional separates. The paprika Liz Claiborne turtleneck sweater and matching sweater jacket allow her ease of movement in working with her four-legged patients, yet they give her lots of polish, especially the lapels and gold buttons on the jacket; the jacket also gives her the benefit of the Rule of Three. The black corduroy pants are practical and flatter her proportions, as the continuous line of black in her pants, hose, and leather loafers balance her rather short legs. The black and paprika scarf pulls the outfit together and adds interest at the neckline, bringing the eye up and adding longitude. To echo the gold buttons on the jacket, we put gold disks at her ears.

Not only does Tené's makeover enhance her stature professionally, her fiancé loved her new, womanly look.

CLAIRE

At thirty-four years of age, Claire (5') handles major responsibilities as a bank vice-president and a single mother. But when I met her, she looked no older than her two teenage daughters. Not only is she petite, she has what she calls a "baby face." And because her figure is proportionately long and lean, she could easily wear inexpensive junior clothes, styled for a younger woman's figure and pocketbook. Claire saved money, but she lost credibility. At work, she usually wore soft dresses that featured a bow at the neck or a slight ruffle, and she wore little makeup.

Previously, Claire hadn't given much thought to her image—"I just got the job done." She requested a makeover because she'd begun to feel that as the only woman in a very competitive environment, her ingénue look was hurting her career. "I felt I have been underestimated many times," she said.

I wanted to make Claire look like the competent executive she is and to bring out the full potential of her beautiful brown eyes and radiant smile.

Her hairstyle, which she'd worn for years, was too casual for her position and too long for her petite frame—it tended to drag her down. So Claire's new sophisticated look started with cutting her hair and giving her a permanent for more height. To accent her features, we lifted the hair off the face with backcombing, blending it carefully. We also highlighted her hair to bring out its gold tones. I was delighted when Claire reported that even her hypercritical teenage daughters liked her new hairstyle!

What Claire called her "baby face," the makeup artist referred to as "the Debbie Reynolds look," suggesting freshness and pep. A light coverup effectively masked the circles under her eyes. We applied a brighter base to counteract the sallowness of her olive complexion, followed by raspberry cheek glow. Burgundy, gray, and taupe shadows were blended on her lids. We also used taupe eye shadow to narrow the bridge of her nose and make her eyes look larger.

Now came the time to add clothes and jewelry to Claire's total look. A muted Chinese-red silk blouse and slim matching skirt (both by Paul Stanley) gave her both the executive attitude she needs for her position and a continuous line of color for lots of longitude. She gained another vertical from the pleats in the blouse.

Claire's slight frame let us break several rules and give her extra flair. First, we chose a snakeskin belt in a contrasting color, gray. With the belt to pull them together, the matching skirt and blouse looked like a dress. Second, we put her in a gray-and-red plaid doubled-breasted jacket (also Paul Stanley) in a longer proportion than many petites could wear. On her, the plaid and layers of fabric provided substance, as well as the Rule of Three.

Sheer gray hose and gray pumps extended the line. We chose *significant* accessories: stunning silver at her ears (which her new hairstyle revealed to perfection) and a silver link necklace to complement the jewel neckline of the blouse (this is one of those necklines that "carries" a short necklace well). An optional piece is a silver lapel pin for the jacket. Claire was intrigued by the polished look created by separates. The key is careful planning of a "total" look, head to toe.

The effect?

Following Claire's makeover, a regular customer at the bank walked by her desk twice without greeting her. After the second time, he finally stopped and said, "It's really you. What happened?"

"Well, I changed my hair," Claire answered.

The man looked at her for a moment, and shook his head. "No," he said. "It's not just your hair. *You've* changed."

RUTH

"My appearance has *everything* to do with how others initially assess my competence," said Ruth (5′) in her request for a makeover.

After raising a family and teaching high school, Ruth returned to college for an engineering degree. She now works for a large corporation as a mechanical engineer. Ruth realizes the importance of a professional appearance and has always worn a jacket at work. Nevertheless, her boss often called her "Kid" or "Little One," and colleagues referred to her as "Shorty." "It generally takes a long time for my co-workers to realize my expertise and value. It took months for me to get significant assignments," she said.

It's never easy being a woman in an otherwise all-male environment. But Ruth's appearance compounded the problem. She made herself virtually invisible by wearing no makeup and dressing primarily in brown and neutral shades. Uncertain as to how to accessorize, she wore no accessories at all. "I work in a very conservative office and I don't need to be real pretty," she said when she came in for her hairstyle.

I set out to convince Ruth that not only could she look "pretty," but that a more vibrant appearance would enhance her professional image.

We started by layering her fine, limp hair and cutting it above her shoulders. We also gave her a body wave and, because she has a small face, swept her hair back at the sides. That brought more attention to her pretty eyes, pert mouth, and dimples . . . as did gray shadow, navy eyeliner, and rose blush. We extended her small mouth just slightly with lip liner and filled in with blue-red lipstick. For a ten-minute daytime routine, we recommended that Ruth skip foundation but use concealer or coverup for blemishes, then add blush, shadow, liner, and mascara. (Ruth went back to the cosmetologist the next week for a more in-depth makeup lesson.)

To help Ruth convey authority, we went for an executive attitude and followed the Rule of Three. We dressed Ruth in a cream silk blouse and a slim navy skirt (both by Anne Klein II), with dark hose and shoes to extend the long line. The *pièce de résistance* proved to be a long, sleek Anne Klein II jacket of deep red. "I've never worn red, ever!" gasped Ruth. On the way to choose accessories—gold love-knot earrings—she stopped and gazed at herself in wonder every time we passed a mirror.

"I look so sophisticated and elegant, so much different from how I'd perceived myself," she said.

Ruth's reaction gave me a warm glow inside. So did what she told me after the makeover. When we first put her in the red jacket, she said she felt "like a million dollars." But she added cautiously, "I'll probably have to work into red gradually. In my line of work, I don't want to come on too strong." Just two weeks later, at a reception to celebrate these "new women," she showed me a smashing red suit she had just bought.

Ruth's husband enthusiastically supports her more vibrant appearance. "She's commanding!" he says.

JAYE

Jaye (5′½″) worked for many years as a legal secretary. Several years ago she returned to school for training in graphic arts, and she now has her own graphic design firm. Despite the flair and creativity I knew Jaye displayed in her work, her appearance lagged behind. She wore her prematurely gray hair in a soft, curly "bubble." The yellowish cast of her hair made her skin look sallow, and both the color and the outdated round silhouette tended to age her. She was overlooking the potential of her eyes: By rimming her upper and lower lids in a dark teal blue, she confined her deep-set eyes; her oversized eyeglass frames, popular in the 1970s, overwhelmed her. Jaye felt comfortable in suits but disliked their consistently conservative look. She showed her artistic nature most in her choice of colors—flattering blues, roses and pinks.

Jaye needed an updated look to match her professional creativity and reflect her vivacious personality.

To begin Jaye's makeover, we changed her hair color to a becoming beige shade. We gave her fullness on top, rather than at the sides, for more height and a flattering oval silhouette. We brought her hair down to lower her forehead and accentuated her cheekbones with soft curls at the sides. I loved the overall effect—younger, softer, more chic—and so did Jaye.

Her "after" eye makeup fills in the lid with mauve shadow and gives the illusion of a narrower nose bridge. We "extended" the eyes at the outer corners with darker gray shadow, thus enlarging and emphasizing Jaye's lovely eyes. We also darkened her brows for more definition. We applied a darker foundation under her jaw to camouflage her neck, which shows signs of thickening with age.

A mature petite, Jaye doesn't need a suit jacket (the Rule of Three) to reinforce her credibility. And as a graphic artist, she can afford some softness, which also gives her a more contemporary image. The dusty pink two-piece sweater dress (by Carole Little) does just that. It's feminine in attitude, yet very professional. The color is becoming and the loose sweater top flatters Jaye's figure, concealing a slight tummy. To give her extra interest at the neckline, we added a paisley blouse under the sweater.

You will notice that we bent a rule in choosing an outfit with a horizontal border around the middle. It works in Jaye's case for several reasons: The pattern is open and extends upward; the pink from shoulder to hem helps compensate for any shortening effect the border may create; and the interest at the neckline balances the outfit, ensuring that the eye comes upward. Jaye also gains style from breaking the rule about pattern mixing, with the paisley blouse and the pattern of the dress.

Jaye was seeking a look with more "flair," and that's what she got. Now she is a walking billboard for her creative, contemporary business. The accessories really give her pizzazz. The silver "comma" at her neck pulls her ensemble together by repeating the shape of the paisley pattern. We selected smaller, simpler eyeglass frames that give soft color to her face and don't distract from her eyes. The earrings are considerably larger than what she had been wearing, and they look just right, especially with a hairstyle that reveals the ear.

OLDER? ... NO MORE SOPHISTICATED? ... YES!

Jaye's makeover made her look younger and softer. But in the case of Claire, Ruth, and Tené, their "after" looks are more mature. We all want to maintain a youthful look—that is, to have soft, clear skin, bright eyes, shiny hair. But we also want that polish and sophistication that tells the world, "I am worth listening to, I can get the job done." As Claire said after her makeover, "I've always thought of myself as if I'm one of my daughters, as one of the girls. Now I feel like I'm the mother. It feels great."

... TO SENSATIONAL

The bare essentials of these Petite Style makeovers were changes in hair, makeup, and clothing. Yet for each of these four women, the transformation went far deeper than mere outward appearance.

As they achieved new sophistication and looked more glamorous, Ruth, Jaye, Tené, and Claire *recognized* how much natural inner beauty they possessed. As Ruth said when she donned her red jacket, "I look so sophisticated and elegant, so much different from how I'd perceived myself."

They not only gained style, they gained confidence. I'm thrilled every time I look at the before and after photos and see the differences. From small and timid poses, they changed to firm stances with shoulders back, radiant smiles, and poise—proof that looking your best makes you feel fantastic.

As you have followed these four makeovers, you've seen how they drew on all of the elements of Petite Style:

✳ We took advantage of *longitude* for looks that flattered their petite frames

✳ We *broke the rules* selectively, to add individual flair.

✳ We chose significant *accessories* to pull ensembles together and create impact.

✳ We used the principles of *wardrobe arithmetic* to build harmonious total ensembles, but we applied them differently to achieve each woman's goals. In the case of Ruth and Claire, we chose an executive attitude and added a third layer (the Rule of Three) to give them maximum authority. Tené was also concerned about credibility, but her job requires relaxed clothes; for her, we followed the Rule of Three, but with a casual attitude. We chose a feminine ensemble *without* a third layer for Jaye, to give her a softer look that suited her as an artist.

✳ We ensured good *fit* by selecting petite-proportioned fashions for all of these ensembles.

✳ We tailored the outfits to each women's individual *proportions.* Ruth's long jacket had a slimming effect. We minimized Jaye's slight tummy and lengthened Tené's legs. And we took advantage of Claire's slightness to break several rules.

✳ We built on their *natural beauty* with hair styling and makeup.

As you are incorporating these principles of Petite Style into *your* look, no doubt you are experiencing an internal transformation as well—feeling excited and energized. The final section of this book, Petite Power, will reinforce those internal changes, as you take command of yourself and the world around you.

Petite Power

Come Across with Authority

CHAPTER
10

Knock'Em Dead

Not long ago, I was invited to do a petite fashion seminar for a department store. I was chatting with the store coordinator, who's quite tall, and she said, "How tall are you anyway? 5'3"?" She was astounded to hear my true height—4'11"!

My experience illustrates one of the great truths about height. When we are children, we learn to associate height with authority: Parents, teachers, doctors are always taller. Our adult minds subconsciously continue to link height and power. Thus, we frequently misjudge others' heights, based on the authority they project. There are dozens of examples of well-known men and women who are habitually perceived as taller than their actual height because they have so much *stature.* Who would ever guess the regal Dolly Parton is a five-footer? or that Humphrey Bogart was just over 5'8"?

Now, I don't give a hoot whether people think I am 4'11" or 5'3". But who wouldn't like to project leadership, credibility, and confidence? All it takes is . . . *presence:*

Project a memorable image when you enter a room.
Reach your audience.
Expand your personal space with effective body language.
Speak well of yourself.
Exercise your authority when you're the boss.
Nip "short jokes" in the bud.
Check up on how you come across.
Emanate greater stature . . . and enjoy it!

Because people perceive me as having *presence,* I literally come across as several inches taller than my actual height. So can any petite. Just as you consciously choose clothes to elongate your appearance, you can use the strategies in this chapter to add inches to your total image.

WOMEN TO LOOK UP TO

"When I first came to New York, I thought I'd never get in the chorus of a Broadway show—the girls are usually tall and leggy," says **Leilani Jones** (5'2"). "Well, I was right! I never did do chorus. I got cast as the *lead* in my first Broadway show!"

Hawaiian-born Leilani is a powerhouse petite. She won Tony, Drama Desk, and *Theatre World* awards for her role as Satin in the Broadway show *Grind*. When she starred in *Shout Up a Morning* at the La Jolla Playhouse, the critics raved. She has also appeared in numerous commercials.

Leilani considers her petiteness a plus. "People sometimes underestimate you when you're small, perhaps because small size is associated with youth. This is an advantage because you are in control of a situation, when the other party doesn't know *who* they're dealing with!"

PROJECT A MEMORABLE IMAGE WHEN YOU ENTER A ROOM

Perhaps more than anything else, countless petites tell me they envy tall women their ability to make an entrance. I know, however, we *can* make a striking impression—whether it's being noticed at a business conference or walking into a swank reception and catching every eye. My secret for making an entrance they'll remember? It's a combination of fashion savvy and Petite Style.

✳ *Wearing a hat* is a sure way to catch an eye at a luncheon, banquet, or evening affair. Even a tam at a casual event will make you noticed. (Of course, by now you know how to choose the most stunning hat—follow the guidelines in the accessories chapter.) Because hats are not common today, many women avoid wearing them. But if you want to stand out, this is one way to make sure you do.

✳ If wearing a hat is not your style, consider the dramatic effect of a beautiful *shawl* draped over one shoulder of your suit jacket and creating gentle ripples as you saunter in with all the insouciance at your command.

✳ Another way to attract attention: Wear a blouse, suit, or dress in an *eye-catching color*—for example, a red blouse under your suit jacket, or the usual tailored suit in an unusual color such as royal blue.

＊ *Unique clothing items* will also command attention in a room full of people. A sweater with a hand-knit texture will be admired and you will be noticed.

＊ Don't make the mistake, however, of thinking that more is better. Sometimes *simplicity* is a singular attraction. As I walk among women bedecked in ruffles, frills, and multiple accessories, I always stand out in a favorite long red knit dress that follows my curves and flares slightly about my knees.

You're strikingly dressed and you're nearing the door! Now *pause* as you enter the room. Not only will you stand framed in the doorway, it's also a good opportunity to scan the room, identify people you want to approach, locate information tables, and so forth. Take a deep breath. Then take purposeful strides—no small, timid steps for you. And, of course, use your smile and handshake to help people remember you.

One last piece of advice: Recognize that there is no turning back. If you're accustomed to entering a room unnoticed, you may feel flustered to be in the limelight. Be prepared for the attention that will come your way . . . and appreciate it.

WOMEN TO LOOK UP TO

Although she's completely at ease at her typewriter, writing the humorous columns carried by nine hundred newspapers, **Erma Bombeck** (5′3″) confesses she's uncomfortable with being a celebrity. "I know that when I walk into a room, I don't stand out. I disappoint people when they see me in person . . . I'm always shorter than they expected. They're so disappointed by my size, they always tell me, 'Oh, my God, I thought you were taller!' So I say, 'Well, I write tall.' " She certainly does. In addition to her popular column, Ms. Bombeck has written seven best-selling books and appears regularly on *Good Morning, America*.

REACH YOUR AUDIENCE WHEN YOU GIVE A SPEECH

Because Nancy (5′4″) knows more about interactive video production than almost anyone in the U.S., she had been invited to speak at numerous conferences. She has developed a terrific strategy to boost her self-confidence on these important occasions. For several days before the speech, she says to herself, *"You're gonna knock 'em dead!"* "I do it while I'm taking a shower and when I'm looking in the mirror and putting on my makeup," says Nancy. "And it internalizes, it really works."

Whether you are going to give a speech, participate in a key meeting, go for a job interview, or make a sales presentation, the following tips will give you *presence* when it counts so much:

Dress with Care

✳ Whatever you wear, purchase or choose it in advance, in case it needs alterations, repairs, or laundering.

✳ Wearing a smashing new suit or dress is a great confidence-builder. But give a new item a trial run, to make sure it's comfortable.

✳ Eliminate anything that might distract from what you say—too busy a pattern, too much detail, or anything noisy, such as bangle bracelets.

Psych Yourself Up

✳ Use Nancy's technique—"I'm gonna knock 'em dead!"—or invent your own. Natasha Josefowitz (5'2"), a nationally recognized authority on women in business, says, "Whenever I'm going to give a speech, I think, 'This is going to be such fun. People are going to love it, I'm going to love it. It will be terrific.' "

✳ A key to confidence is preparation. Think about what you're going to say in advance. Rehearse your opening remarks to help carry you over any initial nervousness. In the case of a job interview, imagine what questions *you* would ask yourself, and practice your responses.

✳ Visualize the event from beginning to end, in advance. See yourself arriving on location, introducing yourself, approaching the lectern, giving the speech (eloquently), returning to your seat . . . and graciously receiving the compliments of the audience afterward!

✳ Another technique: Re-create the good feelings you've had from other successful engagements. Recapturing that sense of satisfaction and exuberance creates a mind-set to do it again.

Make Yourself Visible

✳ Wear something that will attract and keep attention, and make you stand out. For example, professional speaker Patricia Fripp (5'1"), one of our "Women To Look Up To," is noted for the hats she wears. At a job interview or board meeting, wear a bright color near your face, in a scarf or a blouse.

✳ Don't get lost behind a lectern. Instead, stand to the side of the lectern.

✳ Using a microphone? Adjust a floor microphone to your height. When it is just below your chin, it will pick up your words easily and won't obscure your face. Or request a lavaliere-style microphone, which clips to your lapel or goes around your neck on a chain.

✳ In a situation when you are seated, stand up at every opportunity. When someone enters the room, stand to shake hands. Stand to make a comment or ask a question . . . and *project*.

EXPAND YOUR PERSONAL SPACE WITH EFFECTIVE BODY LANGUAGE

I am a firm believer that authority comes from within. Your body language has a great deal to do with your credibility and impact. *How* you say something is almost more important than *what* you say. In the words of the immortal Mae West (5'), "It isn't what I do, but how I do it. It isn't what I say, but how I say it and how I look when I do it and say it." Thanks, Mae. Let's look at four aspects of body language—eye contact, posture, sitting, and gestures—and discuss how to use them to enhance your power.

Eye Contact

When 5'4" vice-presidential candidate Geraldine Ferraro debated George Bush (6'), she stood on a ramp. "The Democrats didn't want him to be looking down at me or, and more important, me looking up at him," says Ms. Ferraro in her autobiography.

Talking to a tall man or woman can be a pain in the neck. Especially if I am standing within arm's length of a tall person, I have to tilt my head just to hold a conversation. After twenty or thirty minutes of this, I may require the services of a chiropractor. So why insist on seeing eye to eye? What's wrong with looking someone in the navel? A lot.

Eye contact conveys confidence, sincerity, and acceptance. Sustained eye contact assures the other person of your full attention. Indeed, the eyes have it! The importance of eye contact in our culture is reflected in our language. Consider these common phrases:

✳ Look up to   ✳ Look down on

✳ See eye-to-eye   ✳ Look straight in the eye

Refusing or ignoring eye contact suggests that you are timid, that you're concealing something, or that you're unwilling to become involved. It also cuts off an important source of information. Eye contact provides you with essential clues about the person to whom you're talking. The eyes show the first signs of illness, anger, fear, boredom, pleasure, or stress. People's eyes often tell you more than their words about how they are responding to you and your ideas.

Unfortunately, establishing and maintaining eye contact means petites must consistently "look up to" others, and they in turn "look down on" us. The potential consequences are more than just neck strain. Disparity in eye level affects your perceptions of yourself and the other person.

As Ralph Keyes points out in *The Height of Your Life*, "Who looks up to whom, who deals eye to eye, and who gets looked down upon are very important issues in our society." He notes that people in positions of power are placed above us, traditionally enlisting the aid of platforms, pulpits, or thrones. They have even required others to curtsey or bow to ensure that the looked-down-upon will have to look up . . . high. Thus, consistently having to look up to maintain eye contact may subtly undermine a petite woman's self-confidence.

So how do you change the balance of power?

✳ Most petites insist on wearing high heels to alter the angle of eye contact. A bank personnel officer told me, "Without my heels, I feel robbed of my authority."

✳ Harriet (5′2½″) suggests maintaining a physical distance from the person you're speaking to—again, to alter the angle at which eye contact occurs.

✳ Another way to avoid looking up—and to give your feet, legs, and back relief from heels—is to suggest that you both sit down. *Sitting is the great height equalizer.* A six-footer towers over a petite woman when both are standing. When seated, their "sitting height" and therefore their eye level are much more consistent. They can "level" with each other. Sitting height refers to the vertical distance from the sitting surface to the top of the head. Since people carry their height primarily in their legs, sitting minimizes extreme differentials in height.

WOMEN TO LOOK UP TO

Like petite mother, like petite daughter . . . at least when they are the multitalented, vibrant Debbie Reynolds and **Carrie Fisher.**

Carrie Fisher has an extra half-inch on her mom. But at 5′1″, she says she's spent her film career staring at actor's chests. The chests include those of Warren Beatty in *Shampoo* and Mark Hamill and Harrison Ford in the blockbuster *Star Wars* films (she played the smart, courageous Princess Leia).

Nevertheless, she has launched a second career as a writer. Her autobiographical novel, *Postcards From the Edge,* was published last year.

I hope that every petite will have the occasion at some time to say, "So this is how it feels!" as she stand among numerous women of her own height. Attending one of our petite fashion shows or seminars is quite a mind-boggling experience for the first-timer. Because she has always looked up to everyone—friends, business associates, spouse, sometimes even her own children!—suddenly gazing eye to eye with everyone around her creates some disorientation at first. It's a heady experience!

Posture

Let me tell you the easiest way to increase your stature: Hold yourself erect. Practicing good posture as you stand and walk will go a long way toward enhancing your attractiveness, your health, and yes, even your height.

Good posture comes from stretching the spine and developing the elasticity of the connecting tissue. That's why people are actually a little taller the first thing in the morning than at night. The weight of the body gradually compresses the connecting tissue of the spinal column through the day. So draw yourself up to your full height in the morning . . . and stay there. By standing tall you give the impression that you are able to handle the day's challenges. (The fact that you'll also look five pounds slimmer is a fringe benefit few of us would refuse.)

I like to keep in mind an image of someone like Olympic gymnast Mary Lou Retton (4'9") standing proudly after her conquest of the vault, or ballerina Natalia Makarova (5'3"), whose presence magnificently fills the stage.

To stand proudly (and beautifully), remember:

✳ Ideal posture starts with a long, stretched neck (the back of your neck, not your throat) . . . as if you're a puppet dangling from a hook.

✳ Your shoulders should be relaxed. Nothing communicates insecurity like shoulders halfway up to your ears.

✳ Descending from your neck, carry your spine as straight and stretched as possible. (Remember the rigid, chest-thrust-forward stance you may have learned as a child? Don't do it . . . unless you're in the Army.)

✳ Tuck your pelvis under you just slightly.

✳ Stand with your knees slightly flexed and feet hip-width apart, with equal weight on both feet and toes pointed forward (the coy, pigeon-toed Betty Boop is *not* your ideal role model).

Next you have to take that well-aligned, stretched body and *move* it. I consulted Judith Greer-Essex (5'4"), who holds an M.A. in dance therapy, for her advice about moving with power.

"Even more than posture, the word 'carriage' to me means how you carry yourself," Judith told me. "It includes the idea of graceful, fluid movement. I like to think of posture as something you work on, but what you're really working toward is a graceful carriage." Carriage

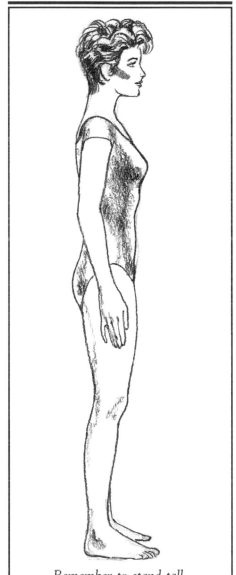

Remember to stand tall.

will indeed enhance your stature. "When people hear how short I am they are generally surprised, because I carry myself tall," she says.

Do you walk fluidly, with strength and purpose? *Stride* is a critical factor in conveying an authoritative image. Some petites shun high heels because they say heels give them a mincing step. Others feel absolutely comfortable in heels and wouldn't give up those long legs and extra inches. Whether you wear heels or avoid them, always aim for a graceful, confident stride.

Sitting

"There's nothing worse than going after that $18-million deal and finding, as you sit across from your client, that your feet are sticking straight out."

DEE, sales representative, 5'1"

Every petite has felt at times like Lily Tomlin doing an impression of "Edith Ann." Comedienne Tomlin brilliantly portrays a small girl who is dwarfed by the adult world, by sitting in a giant rocking chair—it's designed bigger than life-size. Unfortunately, a petite woman often finds ordinary chairs that leave *her* feet dangling off the floor.

Several petites have told me rueful stories about sitting in chairs that were too big for them. Diane, an equipment rental manager who is 5' tall and very slender, drives a thirty-thousand-pound forklift with ease. But she feels uncomfortable in the big chairs at management meetings. Mary (5'½"), a planning commissioner, brings a footstool to long meetings to keep her legs from going to sleep.

It's hard to get others to notice you and your talents when you are virtually lost among cushions or your feet are swinging like Edith Ann's. But you can make choices about where and how you sit that will give you greater authority, even when you can't count on much physical support from your chair.

Is the desk chair in your office proportional to your body, or have you kept the chair left by a 250-pound male predecessor? Go ahead and use cushions to give yourself a little extra height when you're seated behind your desk. (Consider the short man who sawed several inches off the legs of all his guest chairs!) Even better, get your own office chair. On page 142 you'll find detailed information about how to select a chair that fits you properly.

Away from your own turf, if there is more than one type of chair available, select the chair that appears best proportioned to your body. That may mean getting to the board meeting early to get the best seat.

Many petites like to sit with one leg curled under them—a great way to give yourself more stability and height, as long as you're behind a desk. (Don't do it at a glass-topped table!)

If a chair is too big for you, sit on the front of the chair with your feet on the floor. (Think of the strength and reliability we associate with someone who "has her feet on the ground.")

In addition, sitting or leaning forward will score points for you in conversations and other business encounters, as you appear to give your full attention to the speaker and listen intently. Your posture indicates that you have a high energy level, you are receptive to those around you and the ideas they express, and you are willing to cooperate or get involved. Your body language clearly broadcasts, "I am ready for action and able to take charge."

LEFT *For communication confidence . . .*

BELOW *take advantage of your "sitting height."*

Sitting is not a static activity. When you cross your legs, lean forward toward the table, or rest your chin in your hand, your body requires muscular action to maintain balance and stability. If you spend much time sitting, *invest in a good chair*. It will increase your comfort, protect you from back problems, and pay off in increased efficiency. Consider it your "seat of power."

TIPS FOR A PROPER FIT

✳ Principle Number One: Adjustability! Many chairs now have levers that allow you to adjust throughout the day. As you lean forward you can touch a lever that brings the backrest forward with you. You can also adjust the angle of the seat automatically. Whether or not you invest in these features, look for a chair that allows you to alter the height of the seat and the position of the backrest.

✳ If the seat is too high, it will compress the underside of the thigh, restricting circulation and causing discomfort. Recommended seat height: fourteen to sixteen inches off the floor, so your legs can make a ninety-degree angle at hip and knee.

✳ Back support is critical, especially in the small of the back. Avoid a seat that's too deep or a back angled away from the body. You will lose stability and need greater muscular force for balance. No wonder we feel fatigue, discomfort, and back pain!

✳ Arm rests should allow your elbows to rest at a ninety-degree angle, so you don't hunch your shoulders.

✳ Once you fit your chair, you may find, unfortunately, that your chin rests on the table. Raise the seat of the chair so you can work or write at your table, counter, or desk comfortably. You should not have to hunch your shoulders, and you should have sufficient clearance under the table for your thighs.

✳ If the soles of your feet now don't make contact with the floor, use a foot rest (a couple telephone books will do it) to provide stability.

Petite Style

YOUR SEAT OF POWER

The right chair lets you look good and feel great.

Gestures

A gypsy fortune-teller isn't the only person who might anticipate your future by examining your outstretched palm. The way you use your arms and hands communicates whether you feel competent and in control. One can readily detect how a person feels about herself and estimate her status, relative to those around her, by observing her gestures. Does she use them to influence and persuade others as she asserts herself? Or does she distract from her ideas with nervous movements? It's a short step to predicting the kind of opportunities likely to come her way and how she is apt to respond to them.

Space is power. We often attribute authority to large persons by virtue of the fact that they contain more mass. They literally "occupy more space" in the world. *The petite woman can extend her personal space with effective gestures.* Consider the woman who moves her arms freely and naturally, reaching out toward people and objects around her. She exerts her influence and makes herself known to others. Who would dare see the expansive Bette Midler (5'1") or Mae West (5') as powerless!

Gestures can *make* that special difference in how you come across, reinforcing the impression that you are fully in charge. Used poorly, they can also *break* an otherwise strong image. The following dos and don'ts will help you use gestures effectively.

DO

✳ Hold your arms and hands open, relaxed, and unclasped. These gestures suggest you have a similar mental outlook—that is, you are receptive to new ideas.

✳ Be expansive. Put an arm on the table. Pick up a document, a pencil, a file for emphasis.

✳ Use gestures to make points and to focus attention on you and what you have to say.

✳ Extend an arm as a host, to invite your guest to be seated or precede you . . . and to convey the message that you are in control, powerful, and gracious.

✳ Observe other people's body language and trust your instincts. What do you like or dislike about their gestures? What messages do they convey to you?

✳ Take your own natural gestures as your starting point. Pay attention to how you use your arms and hands around your family and friends. Do you notice a difference between those gestures and your body language at work? Experiment with more open mannerisms in an environment where you feel at ease, and introduce them into power situations as you feel comfortable with them.

DON'T

✳ Hold your arms in close to your body—either crossed at your chest or in a "fig leaf" position (clasped in front of your body).

✳ Cover your mouth with your hand(s)—especially when words are coming out!

✳ Hold a hand at your throat. It denotes apprehension.

✳ Preen yourself publicly—patting hair or adjusting clothing or jewelry.

✳ Nervously fidget with your pen, eyeglasses, coffee cup.

SPEAK WELL OF YOURSELF

Few things create the impression of a strong woman who is going to be taken seriously better than do voice and speaking style. You can solve the most common voice problems, to gain both credibility and Petite Style.

It's difficult to hear exactly how you sound to other people, because your voice travels to them through air, whereas you hear yourself through bone. So the first step in building a powerful voice is to record yourself, ideally in a *natural* situation. That is, don't read Shakespeare into the tape recorder, but record yourself in ordinary conversation in your office or on the phone. As you play the tape back, ask yourself the following questions:

✳ Where does your voice fall on a continuum from low-pitched to high? loud to soft? firm to tremulous?

✳ Do you speak slowly and understandably? Or do words often come out in a rush?

✳ Are you blessed with a sparkling laugh or a friendly voice, one that conveys a sincere smile, even over the phone?

✳ Where does your voice rise and fall? Does it frequently go up at the end of sentences, when you aren't asking a question?

✳ How would your voice *read* if you saw it written on a page? Do you have a real knack for presenting information? Do you enunciate clearly? Do you notice frequent "fillers"—*uh, kinda, well, yeah*—or pauses? Do you frequently link sentences together with "and?"

Take note of the things you like and things you'd like to change. You can change them, gradually, by using the following suggestions.

Vocal Quality

A low-pitched, unhurried voice says *you* believe in the importance of what you have to say.

Good vocal quality depends on deep, controlled breathing. If your shoulders rise as you inhale, chances are that your breathing is shallow and lacks control. To improve the quality of your voice, breathe from your diaphragm, exercising your abdominal muscles. Your waist should expand and contract as you breathe.

The pitch of your voice rises (and may become strident and shrill) when you are nervous or trying to speak loudly. Consciously lower your pitch to a *comfortable* level. Let me stress "comfortable." Trying to speak unnaturally low can damage your voice box.

A telephone speaker diminishes the bass in your voice. Before you pick up the phone, take a deep breath and remind yourself to speak in relaxed (lower) tones. (One petite taped a note to her phone that said, "Inhale . . . Exhale . . .")

Smile as you talk. It will come through in your voice even as you speak on the telephone.

Making an important phone call? Stand and gesture as you speak—it will lend vigor and conviction to your voice. (This is a trick all radio actors know.)

Speaking Style

Firmness and clarity are the hallmarks of good speaking style. Be conscious of where your voice rises and falls. Women, especially, have a bad habit of using an upward inflection—as if asking a question or asking permission—at the end of a statement. If *your* voice frequently goes up at the end of sentences, *practice* making declarative statements.

Go a step further and phrase your questions in the declarative whenever possible. You will sound assertive and have greater presence.

Instead of "May I have . . . ?"
say "I would like . . ."
Instead of "Can I exchange this?"
say "I need to exchange this."
Instead of "Can I go home now?"
say "I've finished this project, so I'd like to leave."
Other alternatives to asking questions: "I'd like to clarify what you said." "Refresh my memory on . . ."

Speak firmly and decisively. Vague or tentative statements get less attention. Avoid words and phrases such as, "I think . . . Perhaps . . . It seems to be . . . It is kind of . . . rather . . . somewhat."

Don't trail off at the end of your sentences. What you have to say is important from beginning to end!

If you decide you want expert help, of course, you may consult a speech coach. But most speech problems don't require professional attention. Consider taking a speech course at a local college or joining an organization that specializes in developing speaking skills such as Toastmasters International.

To augment your firm, influential voice, let me share a few conversational power strategies:

✳ Don't just "give up the floor" if someone interrupts you. Maintain eye contact with the person to whom you're speaking and increase your volume slightly. You might use a nonverbal signal, such as raising your hand in a "stop" gesture. Or state firmly, "I'm not finished."

✳ Use the other person's name. Notice name tags on someone's door or desk, or pinned on people's shoulders. Address them by name to ensure their attention and personal involvement.

WOMEN TO LOOK UP TO

If the stereotypical film director is the big, dictatorial man, then **Susan Seidelman** is turning the stereotype inside out and upside down. The 4'11" Ms. Seidelman has established a reputation as one of the most promising young filmmakers—quirky, independent, and brilliant. Her first film, *Smithereens*, cost $2 million to make and brought her to the attention of Hollywood. Her second, the hilarious *Desperately Seeking Susan*, featured pop star Madonna.

On the set, Ms. Siedelman is known for her "strong-willed" authority "Let's face it, I'm not the most imposing figure," she says. "And I'm not one to be coquettish." She described her third film, *Making Mr. Right*, as a "comedy about love from a post-feminist perspective."

✳ You will feel diminished stature if you are called by your first name, yet are expected to call others "Mr. Smith," "Dr. Jones." Put yourself on an equal footing by going to a first-name basis, or by asking them to address you formally, too.

✳ One of the most powerful strategies of all: Be sure to listen when other people are talking, rather than planning what you're going to say next. Your skill in listening will help achieve mutual understanding and shows that you value others' ideas.

EXERCISE YOUR AUTHORITY WHEN YOU'RE THE BOSS

Petite women in management and supervisory positions face the same challenges that confront all women moving into these previously male jobs. *Plus:* Tradition has it that employees "look up to" those who issue directives or make policy decisions. We may even call a boss a "top dog" or "higher-up." When your subordinates may tower over you, employ some Petite Style to reinforce your authority on the job.

✳ Know your stuff. Research the facts and prepare in advance for meetings and presentations.

✳ Take the initiative. Introduce yourself to someone new by standing up and shaking hands. Extend invitations: to your employees, to take part in relevant committees or work groups; to your peers, to get together for brainstorming sessions or for lunch.

✳ Touch people. Management expert Natasha Josefowitz points out that people with power initiate touch toward people with less power: Doctors touch patients, men touch women, bosses touch employees. To remind them of her authority, Natasha especially tends to touch tall men. "I put my hand on an arm, quite strongly, so there's no mistake as to what I'm doing."

✳ Put yourself in the positions generally associated with leadership. Hold meetings on your own turf. Sit at the head of the table or behind your desk. Stand up to address a group.

✳ Look like the boss. Follow the Rule of Three (from Chapter 4, "Wardrobe Arithmetic") in your business wardrobe. Remember that matched suits project a more authoritative appearance than unmatched suits or dresses. Especially on days when you will interview or evaluate employees, lead meetings, or address *your* superiors, dress for credibility.

✳ Apply what you've learned in this chapter. Make the most of your knowledge of body language and voice.

NIP "SHORT JOKES" IN THE BUD

At 58 years of age, Ambassador [Shirley Temple] Black is still possessed with much the same kind of appeal and charm and, oh well, there's no avoiding a certain word here, cute, in a way that's reminiscent of the child film star.

SCOTT SIMON, National Public Radio

When I heard that comment on the radio, I couldn't help but think of some of the stories petite women have told me. "Everyone tells me I'm cute. Who wants to be cute at forty?" lamented Carol (5′).

Women who project the most mature, professional images still say they're occasionally subjected to unwanted comments, and embarrassing situations related to their height. Most of the time, they just laugh them off. The last time I came to the door wearing jeans and my favorite sweatshirt and a teen selling candy asked if my mother was home, I chuckled about it for a week.

How *you* respond to a "short joke" depends on several factors: the nature of the joke; who's delivering the joke—a friend, a spouse, or your boss; the setting—public or private, among friends or at work. Whatever the circumstances, I guarantee that the following suggestions, gathered from my own experience and experiences many petites have shared with me, will help you nip "short jokes" in the bud.

Response #1: Ignore the Joke

Some jokes just don't warrant a response of any kind. They're innocuous, they're made by someone we'll never see again, or we very consciously choose to let them go by.

Sarah (5′2″) dislikes it when her boss pats her on the head, but she ignores it. "There are more important things (more related to being a woman than to height) I've asked him to stop doing, which he has," she explains. Sarah has the *presence* to choose the battles she's going to fight with her boss . . . and this isn't one of them.

Another twist to this strategy: Don't respond directly, but assert your authority immediately. "Male corporate executives often want to play hug and kiss because I'm petite—very patronizing gestures," comments Rhonda (4′11″), a sales manager. Rhonda's solution? "I back away and extend my hand."

Response #2: Humor

Humor is many petites' favorite way to turn the tables on "short jokes." A quick wit lets the joker know he can't intimidate you. And by "taking the floor" with a joke of your own, you put yourself in a position of power; you can change the subject to get on with the business at hand.

Humor also has the power to defuse a potentially tense situation. "I once had a customer (6′4″) lift me up over his head, my arms and feet kicking and flinging around, to show my other clients how 'doggone

148

Petite Style

cute I was.' I told him if he didn't put me down I might be sick all over him." laughs Diane (5'1"). Diane wanted to maintain a friendly relationship with her customers. By using humor, she made the point that she didn't like being picked up, but avoided creating bad feelings in an important business setting.

Every petite I've talked to has her own special "short joke" comebacks. Let me share a few of my favorites.

"I say anyone bigger than me is taking up excess space."

"I'm small, but I'm mean."

"I'm not short, I'm petite. Then they want to know what petite means and they'll learn a new vocabulary word" (this from a teacher).

"When someone asked me if I needed a phone book to sit on, I said I prefer to sit on someone's lap!"

Response #3: Draw the Line

Humor works in many situations . . . but not all the time. If a joke strikes you as cruel or offensive, or if it undermines your authority, you owe it to yourself to draw the line. Earlier I mentioned three factors that will influence how you respond to a "short joke"—the nature of the joke, who's making it, and where it occurs. Particularly when a joke takes place in a power situation and/or public, firmness wins the day.

Margo (5'1") has risen to a top position in her chosen field, radio, by a combination of talent, hard work, and establishing her credibility as a woman in a male-dominated profession. When a man at a crowded social function teased that he was going to pick her up—and actually put his hands around her waist—she didn't want to lose her dignity in front of her peers. Margo said quietly but firmly, "Please don't do that, you're embarrassing me." Then she quickly changed the subject so that *he* wouldn't feel embarrassed and pick her up just to save face.

Ruth (5'), the engineer who is one of our makeovers, was dismayed when her manager called her "Little Missy" in front of her co-workers. She privately asked him not to call her anything he wouldn't call the male engineers. "He respected that," she says. He has treated her with respect ever since . . . and never called her "Little Missy" again.

You've probably noticed that there are two important elements to drawing the line: One is firmly saying what you want. The other is saving the joker from unnecessary embarrassment. Sometimes, I admit, we're sorely tempted to let someone who's made a dumb joke squirm. But usually we have nothing to gain (except an enemy) by humiliating someone else. Margo let her joker "save face." Ruth talked to her boss privately. These very savvy petites exerted their power, and they did it with Petite Style.

CHECK UP ON HOW YOU COME ACROSS

Just as you go to the doctor and dentist for regular health checkups, why not regularly examine how you come across? Do your body language, voice, and appearance promote your image as a stylish, confident woman?

Be honest with yourself. Look in the mirror! Reflect on the feedback you receive from friends and co-workers. You might also enlist a good friend to tell you frankly what your body is communicating, going through this chapter and starring the areas where you'd most like to improve.

EMANATE GREATER STATURE . . . AND ENJOY IT

What a wealth of strategies is at your command! You already know how to *look* your very best. Now you've learned the art of *presence*. You . . .

Project an image that will make heads turn when you enter a room.

Reach your audience, whether it's one thousand people at a conference or *one* prospective boss at a job interview.

Expand your personal space and influence—maintain eye contact, stand/stride with grace and confidence, sit attentively, and gesture for impact.

Speak clearly and firmly, in a low, unhurried voice that lets your listener know you believe in what you have to say.

Exercise the authority that belongs to you when you're the boss.

Nip "short jokes" in the bud through a savvy combination of choosing when to respond to them, calling on your sense of humor, and firmly drawing the line when someone goes too far.

Check up regularly on how you come across.

Emanate greater stature . . . and enjoy it! Just don't be surprised when you knock 'em dead! You're reaping the benefits of coming across with all the Petite Power you possess.

The latter's the one special ingredient that will make *presence* yours forever.

CONCLUSION

Live the Promise

I have had the pleasure of meeting and talking with many of you. I have treasured what you've shared with me, and I've deeply enjoyed getting to know you. I feel I have made a new friend.

As we began this journey to Petite Style, I promised you that every one of you could develop your own one-of-a-kind style. That special style can be yours . . . as you promise to make Petite Style a part of your life.

Style truly can be learned. You have seen how to create looks that flatter you as a petite woman, looks that enhance your figure and express your multifaceted personality. Every time you shop, and every time you put together an outfit, you have an opportunity to practice Petite Style, and to learn more about what it means for you. You will discover the distinctive colors, fabrics, and looks that define your unique style. Just be ready for all the compliments you will receive.

In our journey together, we witnessed four makeovers. We saw each woman blossom as her natural beauty was realized. In the same way, Petite Style will bring out the beauty within you.

As you incorporate Petite Flair, Fit, Polish, and Power into your life, you will discover that Petite Style breeds confidence as well as beauty. With each step you take toward Petite Style, you will feel more assurance, energy, and zest for life.

In the months and years ahead, enjoy your clothes, accessories, and most of all, yourself. Experiment with styles, colors, and silhouettes. Try new fashions. Delight in wearing clothes that fit you better than ever before. Relish your dynamic presence, and continue to grow. Let your sense of style evolve . . . and celebrate it! You have everything you need for lifelong Petite Style.

Appendix

Petite Fashion
Particulars

Scarf-Tying Techniques

✳✳ Wear an oversized square or oblong scarf as a third layer:

1. Drape it over one shoulder; anchor it invisibly with a pin or catch the ends in a belt.

2. Fold a square into a triangle and drape it across your shoulders, with the ends hanging in back or knotted at the back of the neck, forming a soft cowl neckline in front.

LEFT *Add a touch of drama with a scarf over your shoulder.*

RIGHT *Form a soft cowl neckline with a scarf tied in the back.*

3. Fold it into a triangle and tie it around your shoulders; secure it in place with a brooch, as shown on page 42.

✳✳ Turn a scarf into a bow.

1. Select a long, narrow oblong or bias scarf. Loop one end around the other and pull up. This end (A) should be longer than the lower end (B).

2. Form one loop of the bow by doubling up the lower end (B).

3. Drop A down over the front and pull up the second loop of the bow.

4. Make both loops and ends even in length and tighten.

Petite Style

LEFT *A flattering big bow made from a scarf.*

BELOW *Three easy steps to make a perfect bow.*

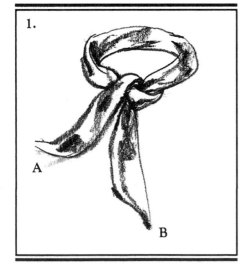

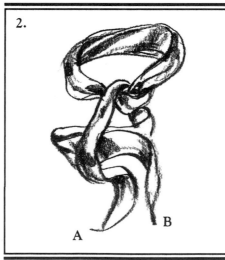

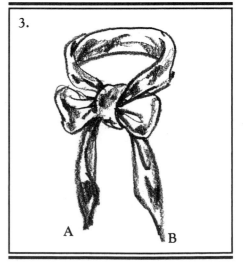

✳✳ Finger-crochet a belt.

1. Take a very long scarf that is narrow and/or of thin fabric, so as to reduce bulk. Make a loop-over knot about four inches from one end.

2. Push a small amount of the long end through the loop, creating a new loop.

3. Repeat the looping procedure throughout the length of the scarf until the belt fits around your waist, leaving enough to tie.

4. Pull the last loop all the way through to secure the knots. Option: With a shorter scarf, make just a few knots in the center of the scarf and tie it around your waist.

Scarf-Tying Techniques

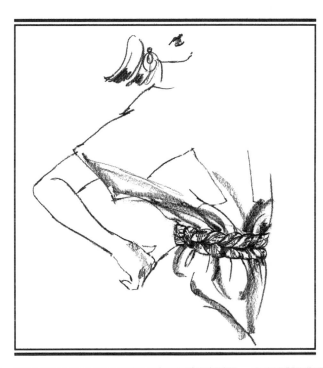

LEFT *Transform a favorite scarf into a new belt.*

BELOW *Three steps to a handmade belt.*

1.

2.

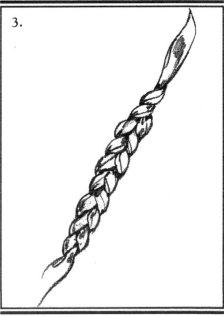

3.

※※ Tie a rosette around your waist.

1. Select a long, narrow scarf and tie it once around your waist, pulling the ends even.

2. Twist the ends together until they coil naturally.

3. Wrap the twisted scarf into a small rosette.

4. Tuck the ends through the center of the rosette from the back.

Option: With a shorter scarf, this may be tied around your neck or head.

158

Petite Style

LEFT *Wear a rosette at your waist.*

BELOW *Four steps to creating a frankly feminine belt.*

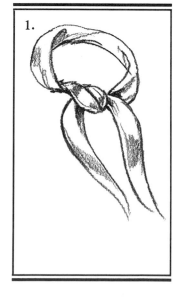

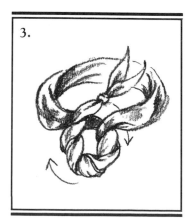

✳✳ Wear a scarf as a necklace.

1. Fold a silk square into a triangle and lay it on a flat surface.

2. Starting at the corner (opposite the fold), fold it over several times toward the folded edge.

3. Gently lift the scarf and loosely tie a single knot at the center.

4. Tie at the back of your neck and tuck the ends under, making sure the knot hangs evenly in front as a "pendant."

LEFT *Jewelry possibilities abound with a folded scarf.*

3.

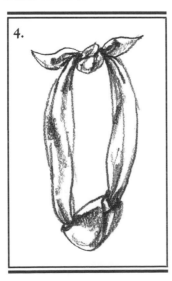

4.

ABOVE *and* LEFT *Two steps to a scarf pendant.*

APPENDIX B

Designer Profiles

LIZ CLAIBORNE

Designer Liz Claiborne sees the "Liz Lady" as a working woman like herself who wants to be "fashionable without being freaky." Liz Claiborne Petites offer the same fashions as the misses lines: Spectator (career), Sport (casual, but can be worn to work), and Lizwear (rugged weekend wear). Petite styles are usually adapted directly from misses, but occasionally the line features a scaled-down version of an oversized jacket, big print, or plaid.

Claiborne clothes are designed to appeal to a broad age range—women aged eighteen and older. "We pride ourselves on the fact that we can service the needs of grandmothers, mothers, and daughters," said sales manager Nancy Worrilow. Tené, in Chapter 9, is wearing Liz Claiborne clothes.

Liz Claiborne introduced petite fashions in 1981. In the future, the company plans to increase the casual and weekend-wear parts of the line.

EVAN-PICONE

Evan-Picone entered the petite market in 1980. Some styles are specifically designed for petites. Others are adapted from Evan-Picone's misses collection, but reproportioned to petite specifications. "Design details such as collars, cuffs, lapels, buttons, zippers, topstitching, etc. are all rescaled," says Larry Lessne, vice-president of Evan-Picone Petites.

Mr. Lessne describes Evan-Picone clothes as "fashionable, functional, comfortable, with a timeless quality." He sees the Evan-Picone

Petite customer as a career woman in middle to upper management. "She prefers and expects quality. She buys tasteful, timeless clothing and rejects trendy, disposable clothes. She is an educated consumer who demands quality and knows and appreciates price value."

LESLIE FAY

One of the first companies to introduce petite fashions (in 1978), Leslie Fay designs specifically for petites, rather than translating from misses designs. "Others adapt misses designs. We have separate lines for petites, because they require something different," company president Mike Fishkind says.

Leslie Fay is known for soft dressing and georgette fabrics. Mr. Fishkind describes the Leslie Fay look as conservative and geared to women thirty-five and older. The company makes four petite lines: Leslie Fay Petite (dresses), Personal Petites (sportswear), Breckenridge Petites (executive fashions), and Summit Sportswear (updated traditional styling). Leslie Fay now has three times the selection it offered three years ago.

ANNE KLEIN II

"Anne Klein II Petites clothing appeals to the petite woman because the styles are sophisticated designer clothing at affordable prices," says Donna Francis, director of public relations. Relatively new to the petite market (introduced in fall 1985), the styles are the same as those in the Anne Klein II collection but are reproportioned for petites.

Anne Klein II Petites feature quality fabrics, including 100 percent linen, cashmere/wool blends, and satin gabardines. The typical customer is seen as successful, aware, motivated, and *busy*; between the ages of twenty-five and forty-nine; and with a household income of thirty-five thousand dollars or more.

For the future, the company's research shows the petite market will continue to be strong. Ruth's ensemble in Chapter 9 comes from Anne Klein II.

CAROLE LITTLE

"We appeal to the petite customer because we offer something not already in the market—a little more fashion," says Anita Benvenuto, sales representative for Carole Little's petite division.

Petite designs are translated from misses. "We work under the concept that the petite woman can wear the same things as the missy, but with balance in mind, as a full jacket paired with a slim skirt," she says.

Carole Little offers petite two lines of better sportswear—Carole Little/St. Tropez West for career looks, and Carole Little/St. Tropez Wear for weekend dressing. Ms. Benvenuto sees the typical customer as a career-oriented woman, twenty-four to fifty-five years old, who is looking for fashion and value.

Jaye's two-piece sweater dress, in Chapter 9, is a Carole Little design.

JONES NEW YORK

Jones New York designs fashions to take a woman "from desk to dinner," says Don Horning, vice-president in charge of sales. "In most cases our customer works, with a good deal of upward mobility—entry level to middle management. She's on the go, and prefers conservative clothing, but with something of a fashion flair." Typical age for the Jones New York clothes buyer is twenty-five and above.

Mr. Horning adds, "She's pretty sure of herself and who she is and wants clothing to stand up to who she is."

At one time, JNY focused on suits. Now it also does softer, more fluid silhouettes. Jones New York petite designs are translated from misses. Petite models are used for seminars in stores. JNY has been in the petite market since 1981. Future plans include offering the Jones Sports line in petites.

ST. JOHN KNITS

Although St. John Knits does not offer a petite line, knits offer more flexibility than cut-and-sewn garments. In addition, St. John provides needed alterations: If a petite needs the fullness of a size 8 but the length of a 6, she can buy the 6 and the company will block the garment to fit.

"We design on a size 8 to 10 model," says Diane Griffith, one of St. John's lead designers. However, Ms. Griffith, (5'1" and a size 2) says she does a lot of designs she feels would look good on herself and would therefore flatter other petites.

"The small woman, to project herself as viable in the world of business, really has to have a nice strong appearance," she says. "But she doesn't have to look like a man in a suit. St. John provides a very colorful, classic garment. That's what I think of when designing. Our clothes look good on a variety of people—it's that good a look, that good a proportion, that good a fit, that makes the garment work."

St. John's Knit sizes go as small as size 2. Among their regular customers is *Today Show* host Jane Pauley (5'3").

PAUL STANLEY

Paul Stanley's petite line uses a mix of styles from the misses line and new styles developed exclusively for petites. Proportions are determined by petite specifications developed since 1981, when the company began designing for petites. ("Paul Stanley is one company who has done their homework in scaling down some great patterns, in jackets specially," says boutique owner Nancy Barisof.)

"We offer fashion merchandise which has not been made available to petites in the past," says sales representative Dennis Olodort. He describes the Paul Stanley petite customer as a successful woman 4'8"–5'4". "She is not a junior-size figure or a shorter-than-average missy—she is a petite. She is looking for fashion and fit, and styling geared to her lifestyle."

Paul Stanley's base fabric is wool gabardine. They also use silk, linen, and novelty fabrics imported from Europe exclusively for their company. In Chapter 9, Claire is wearing Paul Stanley designs.

Petite Style

APPENDIX C

Petite Shopper's Directory

The following list includes petite specialty stores, department stores, and catalogs which offer petite fashions. Catalog addresses are given. In the case of stores, if there are four or fewer outlets, all addresses are given. Large chains are listed giving their corporate addresses and phone numbers, with a list of the cities or states in which outlets are located. You can write or call to obtain specific locations of stores near you. Please be aware that new sources for petite fashions are springing up every year. So in addition to using this directory, check the stores in your local area.

Also in this directory, but listed separately, are sources for small-size shoes and short slips, both of which can pose particular shopping problems for petite women.

In the following list, the letters to the side of each listing designate:
S = specialty store, exclusively for petite women
D = department stores with a special section for petites
C = catalog available

STORES

Abbreviations   S
2423 Westheimer
Houston, Texas 77098
713–523–8663
Boutiques located in Dallas,
Houston, and Austin, Texas.

Barisof   S
606 Pike
Seattle, Washington 98101
206–467–7377

Bonwit Teller **D**
8–10 East 57th Street
New York, New York 10299
212–593–3333
Department stores in Florida, Illinois,
Massachusetts, Missouri, New Jersey,
New York, and Pennsylvania.

The Broadway **D**
550 South Flower Street
Los Angeles, California 90071
213–620–0150
Department stores throughout
Southern California.

Bullock's **D,C**
P.O. Box 91150
Pasadena, California 91109–1150
800–222–9555
Department stores throughout
Southern California and also in
Scottsdale, Arizona and Las Vegas,
Nevada. You can request their
catalog, "Petite Expressions."

Chas A. Stevens **D**
25 North State Street
Chicago, Illinois 60602
312–630–1500
In addition to the petite department
in its State Street store, Chas A.
Stevens has created three petite
specialty stores, listed below.

Chas A. Stevens Petites **S**
Water Tower Place
Chicago, Illinois 60611
312–943–6313

Chas A. Stevens Petites **S**
Old Orchard Shopping Mall
Skokie, Illinois 60076
312–674–8550

Chas A. Stevens Petites **S**
Northbrook Shopping Mall
Northbrook, Illinois 60062
312–498–6264

Chic Petite **S**
239 Crossroads Boulevard
Carmel, California 93923
408–624–4344

Chic Petite **S**
12117 Rockville Pike
Rockville, Maryland 20852
301–984–0310

F B Petites (division of Fashion
Bar department stores) **S**
Cherry Creek Shopping Mall
3030 East 2nd Avenue
Denver, Colorado 80206
303–321–7178

F B Petites **S**
Northglenn Mall
10572 Melody Drive
Denver, Colorado 80233
303–252–0532

F B Petites **S**
Boulder Crossroads Center
1600 28th Street
Boulder, Colorado 80301
303–449–8500

The Great American Short Story **S**
9166 East La Rosa Drive
Temple City, California 91780
800-BE SHORT
Twenty-three stores throughout
California and one in Seattle,
Washington.

The Coat Story **S**
The Cannery
San Francisco, California 94133
415–885–6415
A division of The Great American
Short Story devoted exclusively to
outerwear for petites.

I M Petite **S**
8843 West North Avenue
Milwaukee, Wisconsin 53226
414–453–6644

J.C. Penney Petite Catalog **D,C**
J.C. Penney, Inc., Catalog Division
Atlanta, Georgia
800–222–6161
Send $1.00 for their catalog or call
for the store location nearest you.

Just Petites **S**
Clackamas Town Center
12000 Southwest 82nd Avenue
Portland, Oregon 97266
503–659–2246

Just Petites **S**
275 West Wisconsin Avenue
Milwaukee, Wisconsin 53203
414–271–0467

Karen Austin Petites   S
636 Morris Turnpike
Short Hills, New Jersey 07078
201–379–9000
Forty stores in California,
Connecticut, Georgia, Illinois,
Maryland, Massachusetts, Missouri,
New Jersey, New York, Ohio,
Pennsylvania, Texas, Washington,
and Washington, DC. Two hundred
stores are planned by 1990.

Macy's   D
151 West 34th Street
New York, New York 10001
212–613–1000
Department stores in California,
Connecticut, Florida, New Jersey,
New York, and Texas.

Marshall Field and Co.   D,C
111 North State Street
Chicago, Illinois 60690
800–634–3537
Department stores in Illinois,
Michigan, Texas, and Wisconsin.
You can request their petite catalog,
"Measure for Measure."

Martha's Missy Petite   S
11324 Arcade Drive
Little Rock, Arkansas 72211
501–225–5588

Martha's Missy Petite   S
4556 John F. Kennedy Boulevard
North Little Rock, Arkansas 72116
501–753–7165

Nordstrom, Inc.   D,C
1501 Fifth Avenue
Seattle, Washington 98101
206–628–2111
Department stores in Alaska,
California, Oregon, Utah, and
Washington.
You can request their "Petite Focus"
catalog.

Petite Concepts   S
East Bank Shopping Center
4192 South Parker Road
Denver, Colorado 80231
303–693–4229

Petite Editions   S
Chesterfield Mall
Richmond, Virginia 23220
804–379–2319

Petite Expressions   S
8775 Southwest Cascade Avenue
Beaverton, Oregon 97005
503–644–1414

Petite Expressions   S
11211 Southeast 82nd
Portland, Oregon 97266
503–659–7145

Petite Pleasures   S
1192 Madison Avenue
New York, New York 10028
212–369–3437

Petites and Company   S
Perimeter Mall
Atlanta, Georgia 30346
404–668–0793

Petites by Tangerine, Inc.   S
1702 Merriman Road
Akron, Ohio 44313
216–867–1280

Petite Sophisticate   S
107 Phoenix Avenue
Enfield, Connecticut 06082
203–741–0771
123 stores in 23 states.

Petite Shop   S
24111 Chagrin Boulevard
Cleveland, Ohio 44122
216–831–1128

Petite Suite   S
3961 Palmer Park Boulevard
Colorado Springs, Colorado 80909
303–596–0064

The Petite Woman's Shoppe   S
Water Tower Building
5331 Southwest Macadam Avenue
Portland, Oregon 97201
503–241–8595

Petites West   S
P.O. Box 1872
Fresno, California 93718
209 488–7390
Ten stores throughout central
California

Piaffe   S
841 Madison Avenue, Corner
70th Street
New York, New York 10021
212–744–9911

Piaffe   S
1700 Sansom Street
Philadelphia, Pennsylvania 19103
215–972–1547

Pinstripe Petites   S
Calhoun Square
Minneapolis, Minnesota 55408
612–825–1913
The Pinstripe Petites stores specialize
in career clothes for the petite woman.

Pinstripe Petites   S
Ridgedale Center
Minnetonka, Minnesota 55343
612–545–6363

Pinstripe Petites   S
Southdale Center
Edina, Minnesota 55424
612–925–0081

Pinstripe Petites   S
Rosedale Center
Roseville, Minnesota 55113
612–633–8677

Plaza Petites   S
Chris-Town Plaza
5625 N. 19th Avenue
Phoenix, Arizona 85015
602–242–0798

Plaza Petites   S
Lincoln View Plaza
3151 E. Lincoln
Phoenix, Arizona 85016
602–381–1082

Plaza Petites   S
Loemann's Plaza
1837 W. Guadalupe #106
Mesa, Arizona 85202
602–838–5677

JWRobinson   D,C
600 West Seventh Street
Los Angeles, California 90017
800–777–8910
Department stores throughout
Southern California. You can
request their "Club 5'4"" catalog.

Saks Fifth Avenue   D
557 Tuckahoe Road
Yonkers, New York 10710
800–345–3454
Department stores in Arizona,
California, Connecticut, Florida,
Georgia, Illinois, Louisiana,
Maryland, Massachusetts, Michigan,
Missouri, Nevada, New Jersey,
New York, Ohio, Oklahoma,
Pennsylvania, and Texas.

Sears, Roebuck and Company   D,C
925 South Homan Avenue
Chicago, Illinois 60607
You can obtain a Petites "Specialog"
at your local Sears store.

Serendipity   C
P.O. Box 27500
Tucson, Arizona 85726–7500
800–972–1000
Catalog which includes petite
fashions, as well as shoes starting
with size 4.

Spiegel, Inc.   C
P.O. Box 7623
Chicago, Illinois 60680
800–345–4500
You can request their catalog,
"Proportion: Petite," for coats,
lingerie, accessories, and clothes.

Talbots   D,C
164 North Street
Hingham, Massachusetts 02043
800–225–8200
Department stores in 25 states.
You can also request their catalog.

Talbots' Petite Collection at
Charles Square   S
20 University Road
Cambridge, Massachusetts 02138
617–576–4791
A special Talbots store devoted to
petite fashions.

SHOES

Chernin's   S,C
1001 South Clinton
Chicago, Illinois 60607
312–922–5900
They carry sizes 4 medium and up.
You can call or write for a catalog
or to obtain store locations in the
Chicago area.

Cinderella of Boston, Inc.   S,C
P.O. Box 7110
8607 Canoga Avenue
Canoga Park, California 91304
818–709–1133
They carry sizes 1½ to 5. You can
visit their Los Angeles-area showroom
or request a catalog.

Giordano's   S,C
1118 1st Avenue
New York, New York 10021
212–688–7195
They carry sizes 4 to 6 medium, 5½
to 6½AA, and occasionally size 3. A
catalog is available for $2.00.

Élite Petite   S,C
11441 Stemmons Freeway, Suite 233
Dallas, Texas 75229
214–241–7307
You can request their catalog of shoes
in sizes 2 to 5½.

SLIPS

Barbizon makes a "Snip-It" Petti slip in cotton batiste. You cut off a row of lace at the hem of this half-slip to make it the right length—29, 27, or 25 inches. Available in department stores.

Piaffe offers a half-slip with embroidered lace hem in 21″ or 23″, made of non-cling nylon-blend crepe remarque—nude, white, or black. Available at Piaffe stores in New York and Philadelphia. See the Piaffe listing earlier in the directory.

The following half-slips come 21″ from waist to hem and are available in department stores:

Vanity Fair three-gore style #11711 in 100 percent nylon tricot—in black or white.

Vassarette "Frankly Feminine" side-slit style #5816 in 100 percent nylon tricot—in black, nude, or white.

Olga slit slip, which can be worn front, back, or side. Style #2360, in non-cling polyester taffeta—in nude or black.

One last hint: Take advantage of times when miniskirts are in style to purchase slips that will work under your shorter skirts.

APPENDIX D

Wardrobe
Arithmetic Charts

PUT IT ALL TOGETHER WITH PETITE STYLE

Skirt/Pants	Blouse/Sweater	Rule of Three: Sweater/Vest/Jacket	Shoes	Accessories: Jewelry/Scarf/Stockings	Comments:

PUT IT ALL TOGETHER WITH PETITE STYLE (cont.)

Skirt/Pants	Blouse/Sweater	Rule of Three: Sweater/Vest/Jacket	Shoes	Accessories: Jewelry/Scarf/Stockings	Comments:

PUT IT ALL TOGETHER WITH PETITE STYLE (*cont.*)

INDEX